Tempus ORAL HISTORY *Series*

voices of
Benslow Music Trust

Mary Ibberson, 1950.

Tempus ORAL HISTORY *Series*

voices of
Benslow Music Trust

Compiled by
Margaret Ashby

TEMPUS

First published 2000
Copyright © Margaret Ashby, 2000

Tempus Publishing Limited
The Mill, Brimscombe Port,
Stroud, Gloucestershire, GL5 2QG

ISBN 0 7524 2048 8

Typesetting and origination by
Tempus Publishing Limited
Printed in Great Britain by
Midway Clark Printing, Wiltshire

Cover illustration: *Founders' Day Concert, 1955.*

Other books by Margaret Ashby:

The Book of Stevenage
The Book of the River Lea
Forster Country
Stevenage: History and Guide
Stevenage Past
A Hertfordshire Christmas
Stevenage Voices

Contents

Introduction

This book has its origins in a ploughed field! In 1997, Anne Conchie, a Benslow Music Trust council member, was walking beside me along a muddy footpath, as we took part in a march to save the Forster Country, in north Stevenage, from being built over. Anne inevitably began talking about Benslow and the matter that was currently exercising her mind, the future of its archive. 'You must come and see what we've got in the cellar,' she concluded. So I came and was impressed by the extent of the collection, excited at was revealed by a random opening of boxes and folders, but aware of imminent claustrophobia.

The next question was, 'How can we make the contents of the archive more available to members?' The answer seemed to be that there was more than enough material for a book and a unique story to be told and, somewhat to my own surprise, I undertook to write it. But archives alone could not adequately reflect the infinite variety that was and is Benslow Music Trust. People, living and dead, are its essence, and for over two years I have talked to a great number of the former and I still have only touched the tip of the iceberg. The number and range of people connected with Benslow is truly amazing and I am only sorry that there are so many I have not been able to meet, or whom I have met only very briefly.

When I began the book, it was very much a step into the unknown, but in faith that the right publisher would be found in due time. I am very happy that David Buxton, of Tempus Publishing Ltd, has undertaken the book as part of his Oral History series, because it allows the voices of those who have made Benslow what it is to speak through the pages.

As my research progressed, I began to realise the vastness of the Benslow Music Trust's sphere of influence, a complex, interconnecting network of professional musicians, amateur performers, paid staff, volunteers, local audiences, educationists, national and international supporters and the thousands of people who, as children, were introduced to music in schools throughout the country, as a direct result of the Rural Music Schools Movement.

The story moves from Mary Ibberson's local village classes in the 1920s, through a time of steady expansion culminating in national prestige, followed in the late 1970s by turmoil and conflict over an uncertain future, which in time gave way to rebirth, regeneration and ever-widening opportunities .

I hope that this book will serve as an introduction to the Benslow Music Trust, as a celebration of its achievements and above all, as an acknowledgement of the many, many people who have contributed over the years to this unique movement.

The passages in the book which are direct quotations from other people's written or spoken words are in italics, followed by the name of the speaker or writer.

Margaret Ashby
March 2000

Acknowledgements

A great many people have helped me during my two and a half years of research for this book. The following kindly lent photographs, supplied information or gave practical help: Juliet Abrahamson, Carole and Tony Aston, Dorothy Berry, Bernard and Nona Blay, Elizabeth Black, Anne Conchie, Donald Clark, Stephanie Cooksley, Jenny Dann, Grisell Davies, Howard Davis, Scilla Douglas, Phyllis Ebsworth, Roy Evans (Warden of the Letchworth Settlement), Dawn Fry, Betty Game, Doris Gare, Norma Gillott-King, Sarah Graham, Hertfordshire Archives and Local Studies staff, Hitchin Museum staff, Steve Hodges, Daphne Hope, Olwen James, Helen Jarvis, Joan Jelliffe, Stella Kestin, Jean Laidlaw, Doris Lake, Anne Macnaghten, Ruth Maguire, Helen Marshall, Eileen Maylin, Jean Middlemiss, Robin Miller, Leslie Minchin, David Moore, Sylvia Norman, Francis and Iris Oakes, Anne Parker, Bernard Parris, Kay Petrie, Brenda Roffey, Linnaea Walker, Richard Wiggs.

I am extremely grateful for all the time spent talking to me, writing letters, telephoning and giving encouragement and unspoken support. Please accept my thanks, especially if you are one of the many not mentioned here by name. Your help is no less appreciated.

Photographs. Despite my best efforts, I have not been able to trace the copyright owners of many of the photographs, or to identify many of the photographers.

Bibliography

Bradbrook, M.C. *That Infidel Place – a short history of Girton College, 1869-1969*. Chatto & Windus 1969.

A.W. Brunt, *Pageant of Letchworth, 1903-1914*, Letchworth Printers Ltd, 1942.

Ekwall, E. *Place-names of Hertfordshire*.

Glendinning, Victoria, *A Suppressed Cry; life and death of a Quaker daughter*. Routledge, 1969.

The Hertfordshire Express (file at Hitchin Museum).

Hine, Reginald, *History of Hitchin*.

Hine, Reginald, *Hitchin Worthies*.

Ibberson, Mary, *For joy that we are here*, Bedford Square Press, 1977.

Jelliffe, Joan, *The Story of Little Benslow Hills*, Benslow Music Trust, 1997.

Latchmore, E. Aillie, *People, places & pastimes of Hitchin*,1974.

Minchin, Leslie, *My Footsteps through the century*, 1997.

Walmsley, Robert, *Around 1919, Boyhood Memories of Hitchin*, 1979.

CHAPTER 1

A Hill and its Buildings

Fairfield (Little Benslow Hills), 1860s. (Courtesy Hitchin Museum)

The House

Little Benslow Hills on a December evening at the end of the twentieth century. A visitor walks up to the house, aware of shrubs and trees receding into the surrounding darkness, their branches whispering in the chill wind. Ahead is brightness, shining from windows and from a Christmas tree glimpsed in the hall. The visitor rings the bell, the front door is opened and an appetizing smell of good food wafts into the night air.

In the dining room, people are gathering, exchanging delighted greetings. Tonight is the first night of their course: players from all over the country are happy to be together again, to meet new friends, to share in making the music they love. The staff go swiftly about their work, smiling when spoken to, efficient and kindly.

The visitor wanders into the bar. Here, the curtains are pulled, the light is soft and in the bare hearth is a jug of Chinese lanterns, illuminated by Christmas lights in the chimney. Coffee cups wait on the tables, a jar of biscuits on the mantelpiece.

In the hall is the Christmas tree, brilliant

William Ransom in his garden at Fairfield (Little Benslow Hills). (Courtesy Hitchin Museum)

with candle bulbs and shining, miniature, musical instruments. The visitor, drawn by the red glow of an open fire, sinks on to a large sofa, dreamily aware of holly and tinsel, of the muffled chink of cutlery and the murmur of conversation.

A bell rings. Two late arrivals are welcomed. Office and kitchen staff move into action, there is talk and laughter. The two newcomers scan the course notice board, 'Oh, Lewis is here – and Claire – and...'

Pleased smiles. They stagger upstairs with their instruments. 'Hi, there!'

'Who's that?'

'Paul.'

'Great – this is great.'

After dinner, there will be music...

This house, now known as 'Little Benslow Hills' – and it still has the atmosphere of a house, rather than a 'college' or a 'school' – was built in 1859 by William Ransom, who gave it the name 'Fairfield'. Subsequently he made

alterations and improvements, including, in 1883, an extension to the east side and replacement bay windows in the large south-facing rooms. Ransom, founder of the famous Hitchin pharmaceutical firm, William Ransom & Son, was a Quaker, a wealthy man, hardworking and devout. Fairfield was set in the midst of extensive gardens and surrounded by fields where belladonna and lavender was grown for the business, of which it has been said, 'It combined tradition and technology'.

Poppy petals

Imagine collecting rose-hips, splitting them to get rid of the fibres, or worse still, imagine picking poppy petals and having them weighed. Elderflower gathering was relatively simple, but washing roots under Queen Street conditions was bad and the little courts were often wet. But root-gathering and poor homes went together and when you were unemployed you could obtain pence from working in the lanes.

When a farmer tried to cash-in on the demand for dandelion roots by taking a cartload to Ransom's he made no sale and was obliged to take them back. You see, Mr Ransom thought that the money he was paying out was of more use to the poor who could have been really worried when they found some of his requirements satisfied by those who were not in need.

Robert Walmsley, (Around 1919, boyhood Memories of Hitchin)

A Golden sovereign

Mr Ransom was in the habit of giving a golden sovereign to the children of the staff at the works at Christmas and on one occasion he gave me one and he said he would like me to call and see him at his home at Fairfield and tell him how I had spent his gift. I had just commenced at boarding school at Ackworth School, near Pontefract, at the time and wanted a hockey stick very much. At that time a really good one cost seventeen shillings and sixpence so I bought one with Mr Ransom's gift and the remaining half-crown I spent on a book. In due course I visited Fairfield and told Mr Ransom of my purchases. How well I remember his reply in the old Quaker form of speaking. 'Thank ye for telling me how thou hast spent thy pound but I think it would have been better for thee hadst thou spent two shillings and sixpence on the hockey stick and seventeen and sixpence on a book.'

E. Aillie Latchmore (People, Places and Pastimes of Hitchin)

Benslow

The hill on which Fairfield was built was recorded as far back as 1556 as 'Benchelowe Piece', just outside the town of Hitchin. By 1860 it had become known as 'Benchley' or 'Benslow' Hill. On this same hill, almost opposite Fairfield, but on the other side of the lane, lived William Ransom's brother, Alfred, in his house which was called, more logically, 'Benslow House.'

Two Brothers

One true anecdote about the brothers came up if townspeople called at William Ransom's house to ask for a subscription to some good cause. He would tell the caller to go first to his brother and tell him that whatever he gave, he, William, would double the amount. This caused Alfred, considerably less rich than his brother, to give as much as he could to make his brother, William, give even more than he intended.

E. Aillie Latchmore (People, Places and Pastimes of Hitchin)

That Infidel Place

Alfred Ransom's house, Benslow, just across the lane from Fairfield, is the building where, in 1869, Miss Emily Davies founded this country's first Ladies' University College. A leading campaigner for women's right to vote and especially for their right to education, Emily Davies began her life's work with five students at her Hitchin College. One reason for choosing Hitchin was its location between London and Cambridge, a convenient place for visiting lecturers to come by train. The building at Benslow was within walking distance of the railway station which opened in 1850.

'Ha! this is Hitchin, and that, I believe, is the house where the College for Women is:

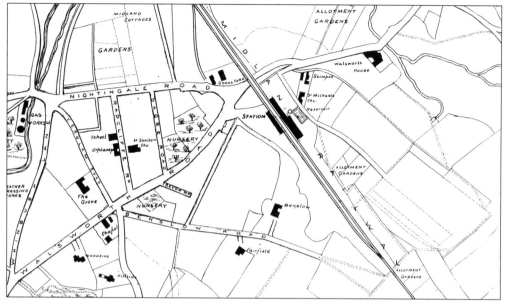

Street plan of Hitchin (late nineteenth century) showing Benslow House and Fairfield (Little Benslow Hills).

that infidel place!' This comment from a railway traveller passing through Hitchin in 1869 gave M.C. Bradbrook a title for her history of Girton College. In it, she describes, through the eyes of the young Quaker, Anna Lloyd, what life was like at the Ladies' University College.

Quaker Hitchin

Although the thought of higher education (or even education) for women was anathema to many in the mid-nineteenth century, there were others, including eminent academics such as John Stewart Mill and Henry Sidgwick, who were ardent supporters, and in five years, Emily Davies' little college had flourished sufficiently to move, in 1873, to Girton on the outskirts of Cambridge and eventually to achieve full recognition as a highly respected college of Cambridge University.

After the departure of Miss Davies and her

students, the building known as Benslow was a maternity home, where many babies from the whole of North Hertfordshire first saw the light of day. It is now a nursing home for the elderly.

Among the supporters and benefactors of Miss Davies' University College were several Quakers, including Frederic Seebohm. The lives of the Hitchin Quakers were closely interwoven. The Tukes lived in Bancroft almost opposite the Ransom factory, close to the Seebohms at the Hermitage. At 74, Bancroft was another Quaker family firm, that of G.W. Russell & Son whose business was leather dressing. Quakers have been prominent in the history of ninteenth- and twentieth-century Hitchin, and in the story of the Benslow Music Trust. Hertfordshire and Bedfordshire have attracted Quakers since the early days of the movement and in 1655, George Fox, the founder, visited the towns of Hertford, Baldock and Hitchin.

Until 1839 the Hitchin Quakers met in premises in Quakers' Alley, now known as

West Alley. In 1840 they were able to build a new Meeting House at the top of Brand Street (now Centenary House) with a burial ground opposite. In 1959 this was replaced by the present Meeting House built over the Burial Ground. Locally there was hostility towards Quakers, even from other puritanically minded dissenters, including John Bunyan. The early Quakers dressed very plainly and conducted themselves modestly, which irritated other people. In Hitchin and elsewhere they were sometimes attacked on their way to the Meeting, or had their Meeting Houses damaged. However, they were involved in trade and their very strict code of practice, their honesty and efficiency gradually earned them the respect of others.

Given the number of wealthy and conscientious Quakers in nineteenth-century Hitchin, it is not surprising that the town had a Quaker school, Isaac Brown's Quaker Academy, situated at Bull Corner, where Queen Street and Bridge Street meet. The education offered must have been of a fairly high standard, as families from other parts of the country sent their sons there. One of these was Joseph Lister, who arrived in 1838 aged eleven, and stayed until 1841. During his years at the Academy he became friendly with another pupil, the young William Ransom, who grew up to found the pharmaceutical firm, and to build Fairfield.

Joseph Lister became a great surgeon and the discoverer of antiseptic. The building in which he attended school is now known as the Lord Lister Hotel and the hospital for north Hertfordshire, the New Lister Hospital at Stevenage, is named after him.

Of all the Quaker community, it is perhaps Frederic Seebohm who made the most continuing and visible impression on the face of Hitchin.

He and his wife Mary Ann, with their family of five daughters, Juliet, Esther, Winnie, Freda

Hitchin Ladies' College, c. 1868. The building is now Benslow Nursing Home. (Courtesy Hitchin Museum)

Fairfield (Little Benslow Hills), 1860s. (Courtesy Hitchin Museum)

and Hilda and one son, Hugh lived in Bancroft, at the Hermitage, a house made up of buildings of various ages. The garden of the Hermitage covered seven acres and extended to Windmill Hill and adjacent woods. A special feature were its trees, notably some of the tallest box trees in the county. Seebohm gave up the south side of the garden to allow Hermitage Road to be built in the 1870s, a great asset to the town as it provided a route from Bancroft to and from the railway station.

Frederic Seebohm

By the furtherance of education, in the fullest sense of that word, he sought to confer on others the qualities he so richly enjoyed. For years he laboured with his friend and fellow Bradfordian, William Edward Forster, to prepare the way for the

Education Act of 1870; for years he laboured to ease the working of that Act, in all parts of the county.

Reginald Hine (Hitchin Worthies)

Hitchin Grammar Schools

Seebohm was a leading spirit in reforming the seventeenth-century Hitchin Grammar School foundation in 1888. Twenty years later, with typical generosity, he gave land on Windmill Hill to build the new Girls' Grammar School. His own daughters had been well-educated at home yet, in spite of his support for Emily Davies' Girton College, he would not allow his delicate and asthmatic daughter, Winnie, to attend. Only after repeated pleas did he give in and agree to her going up to Cambridge in 1885, not to Girton but to Newnham, which seemed to offer a gentler regime more suited to a young girl in poor health. Sadly, Winnie Seebohm enjoyed only fleetingly the higher education she so longed for. Her story is told by her great-niece, Victoria Glendinning:

A Suppressed Cry

Winnie's asthma was getting worse not better, and no improvement could really be expected in other ways while she was so continually racked and exhausted. It was suggested that the low-lying situation of the Hermitage was to blame. William Ransom… who had lost his wife earlier in that same year, suggested that she might benefit from the higher ground of his house, Fairfield. On December 9 [1885] she was driven to Fairfield from the Hermitage, and installed – rather unimaginatively – in the big front bedroom that had formerly been Mrs Ransom's. The change had an effect in that she enjoyed at least two asthma-free nights. But there was no improvement in other ways... she gently ceased to breathe at about four o'clock in the afternoon of Friday, December 18th 1885.

Victoria Glendinning (A Suppressed Cry; Life and death of a Quaker daughter, 1969)

Death of William Ransom

William Ransom died at Fairfield, aged ninety-one on 1 December 1914 and his son Francis allowed the house to be used as a convalescent home for war wounded servicemen during the First World War, financing the operation himself. Ironically, a few hundred yards away, at the top of the hill, was a building known as the German Hospital, which had been built in 1908 and opened in the presence of Princess Louise of Schleswig Holstein, a German baron and baroness and a number of Hitchin worthies:

'Handsome New Building at Hitchin'

The opening of the new German Convalescent Home at Benslow, in connection with the German Hospital at Dalston took place on Saturday afternoon. About 90 guests were present, including Sir Hermann Weber, Sir Julius Wernher, Bart., Baron and Baroness Bruno Schroder... Mr C.J. Grellet (who has kindly accepted the post of Hon. Medical Officer to the Home), Dr W. Engels... Mr Lawson Thompson, Miss Thompson, Mr W.O. Times, Mr W. Ransom, Miss Ransom, Mr F. Seebohm, Miss Seebohm, Mr T. Ransom, Mr R. Shillitoe... the Matron, Sister Elise Jurcke and several Sisters from the hospital...

Hertfordshire Express, 18 July 1908

Little Benslow Hills

In 1912, Frederic Seebohm died and was deeply mourned. Hitchin's historian, Reginald Hine, records that the distinguished Oxford scholar, Sir Paul Vinogradoff, said to him, 'If your town had produced Seebohm and nothing more, it would still deserve its history.' Mrs Seebohm had died nine years previously, Juliet and Hugh had both married and by the end of the First World War, only Esther and Hilda remained in the family home, the Hermitage. It was far too big for them and in 1925 the two sisters bought Fairfield, the former home of William Ransom, now re-named 'Little Benslow Hills,' after the old field name for the site.

Nurses at the German Hospital, 1908. (Courtesy Hitchin Museum)

CHAPTER 2

Mary Ibberson's Inspiration

Letchworth Garden City

A few miles from Hitchin, and administered by the Hitchin Urban District Council, was the tiny village of Letchworth which became, in 1903, the site of an early experiment in town planning. As Ebenezer Howard's vision of a garden city was realised, the population increased from less than 400 in 1903 to over 7,000 in 1921, by which time Letchworth had been constituted, in 1919, an Urban District in its own right.

Quaker Traditions

One of the parishes now included in the civic parish of Letchworth (Norton) had Quaker traditions, indeed North Herts. was in itself the home of many early members of the Society of Friends. It was not strange, therefore, that Letchworth should quickly gather to itself many adherents of this body, a goodly number of whom were active in the very early days and in 1908, through the generosity of Miss Julia Reckitt, Howgills, that very characteristic meeting place was opened and became a centre of the many social and religious activities of this virile body.

A.W. Brunt (Pageant of Letchworth)

Decision by Referendum

It had been decided by referendum that the new, ideal town should be teetotal, contrary to the wishes of Ebenezer Howard himself who, although against the evils of alcohol, said in 1906, 'They must not drive evil into neighbouring towns and villages, but deal with it themselves.' As a result of the referendum a rather unusual public house, the Skittles Inn was opened in Nevells Road, in March 1907, serving only non-alcoholic refreshment.

George Bernard Shaw at Letchworth

G. Bernard Shaw spoke at a Letchworth meeting in March 1907 and said, 'Garden City revealed a peculiar situation politically – it had neither Liberal nor Conservative traditions, and in this respect it is quite different from the usual country town... Garden City was to some extent the outcome of Socialism, and for that reason he had himself invested in the scheme.'

A.W. Brunt (Pageant of Letchworth)

The Letchworth Settlement

Education was high on the agenda of many residents and as early as 1907 people were talking of 'a seat of learning' perhaps to be called 'Howard College.' The hopes for a university did not materialise. Instead, an institution which has served Letchworth and district well and continues to flourish today, was set up by 'A small group of people [who] were moved to form the Letchworth Settlement'. They were inspired by a national Quaker movement, the Educational Settlements Association, to make provision for the further education of adults.

The first warden, James Dudley, and his wife, did much to establish the ethos of the movement. Classes were offered in a number of subjects, beginning with history, literature, economics, science and the appreciation of music. The tutor for music was Mary Ibberson, a young Quaker convert, recently returned from her studies abroad.

A Bewildering number of activities

After studying French in Lausanne I had gone in 1911 to Dresden to study German and piano for a year, and stayed for two more years to work at the Conservatorium... Back then, to England in 1913... and to the early, idealistic days of Letchworth, which... had a bewildering number of activities very attractive to a young woman in her twenties... the women's suffrage movement which gave me some practice in public speaking: and above all Girl Guides... Work with my own companies and, further afield as county camp adviser and trainer of guiders, gave me invaluable *experience in organisation and widened my personal contacts... I was appointed, first as tutor-in-training and, later, as sub-warden of the Settlement,*

Mary Ibberson (For joy that we are here)

Village Classes

The Settlement's published syllabuses show that Mary Ibberson undertook quite a daunting programme of work. The Settlement did not confine its classes to Letchworth, but sent tutors into the villages of North Hertfordshire and South Bedfordshire, often in the evenings, to meet the needs of rural communities. In those days very few people had motor cars, although branch-line trains and some bus services did exist. Music classes were some of the most popular and successful.

A Network of Supporters

There was an increasing network of friends and supporters, such as Edith Grubb, Hugh Seebohm, and Mrs Pryor who not only played her part as a tutor, but also opened her house at Weston for social gatherings and meetings.

As the Settlement's work expanded the need to acquire premises of its own became obvious. The 1924-5 Annual Report states... 'when the Skittles Inn came into the market Council felt it must be secured for the Settlement at all costs'. In November the Council's offer of £2,000 was accepted by the owners of the Skittles Inn and in March 1925 the Settlement took possession of its new home.

Settlement Chamber Concerts

Although her duties as sub-warden were giving Mary Ibberson an increasingly diverse experience of managing an educational institution, it was in the sphere of music education that she made her greatest contribution. In addition to her teaching duties at Letchworth and in the villages, she ran a series of Settlement chamber concerts, drawing in such excellent local performers as Miss Katherine Tudor-Pole, violinist from Letchworth, Miss Edith Grubb, 'cellist, and the warden, himself, James Dudley, who played the violin.

Brass Candlesticks

The last Chamber Concert of the season was given at the Settlement on April 5th... It is not easy to guess just why the workers do not take advantage of the opportunity to hear good music. Is it because there is no musical training, other than vocal, at the Council Schools? Is it because of the bourgeois atmosphere which, to the regret of the staff and of all interested in education, clings persistently to the Settlement? Possibly, though the effect is not only very pleasing but also restful and grateful, it has been a mistake to attempt artificially to recapture the atmosphere of Vienna and Weimar with the aid of brass candlesticks.

Report in 'The Worker', February 1924

A Galaxy of Stars

Mary Ibberson's work for the Settlement was drawing together a committed group of talented musicians, all of whom shared her ideals of bringing good music-making within the reach of everyone. She was also extremely fortunate in attracting to the Settlement professional performers of high calibre, especially Mrs Clarence Elliott, the former Phyllis Eyre. Clarence Elliott, Phyllis Eyre's husband, was himself becoming something of a celebrity as an Alpine plant specialist. His Six Hills Nursery at Stevenage and his plant-hunting expeditions in Europe and America brought him to the notice of other alpine gardening enthusiasts, including the Bowes Lyon family at St Paul's Waldenbury. He was extremely proud of his wife's musical talent and encouraged her in her work. In the Elliott family, the Settlement and Mary Ibberson, had gained not one, but a galaxy of stars.

A Letchworth Gathering

It was indeed a foretaste of 'Merry Christmas' last Saturday evening at the Educational settlement, Nevells Road. The occasion was the Christmas Party to wind up the term. The big Christmas tree was lighted and all gathered round and sang carols under the direction of Miss Ibberson, the indefatigable, who accompanied on the piano, with Mr Dudley's help on the violin.

Letchworth Citizen (24 December 1925)

Why not start a Music School?

The idea of a music school came to me one day when I was reading a report of the successful Neighbourhood Music Schools in some of the big cities of America, and I read it with increasing excitement. These schools were for poor children and fees were adapted to their ability to pay. The qualified professional teachers – working together as a team – were paid, but not necessarily at the top rates. A great deal of voluntary help was given, and money was raised through voluntary subscriptions. At once the thought came – 'If music schools for poor children can be successful in American cities, why not start a music school for adults living in the country in England?'

Mary Ibberson (For joy that we are here)

Birthday Party

28 March 1928. Miss Ibberson's birthday party. A large body of old friends met to bring their birthday greetings and to mark their appreciation. The 'Little Orchestra' played and solos were given by Mrs Swann and Mrs Clarence Elliott – a most successful and enjoyable afternoon.

Settlement Newsletter, May 1928

A Period of Study

The greatest need of all was that I should have a period of study in order to acquire a wider knowledge of the instruments of the orchestra, choir training, arranging simple music for elementary orchestras, and conducting. The Settlement Council allowed me to take a term's leave... My mother, with whom I lived, was an invalid, but she was always keenly interested in what I was trying to do and was an ardent supporter of the Settlement. She willingly agreed to spend three months in a nursing home so that I could go away and study...

The distinguished violin teacher, Miss Editha Knocker... had her own violin school

Mary Ibberson conducting.

in London and Edith Grubb suggested that I should consult her. I saw Miss Knocker in April and she offered an intensive course in her school, specially planned for me. It was to include conducting and elementary violin with her, orchestration and score-reading with the pianist Max Pirani (a most stimulating and entertaining experience) and instruction in wind instruments from a fatherly and encouraging ex-army bandmaster, Mr J. Prosser.

Mary Ibberson (For joy that we are here)

Editha Knocker's Influence

Editha Knocker adjudicated at competitive music festivals throughout the country and she

realised how low the standards were. Her influence in the RMSA helped to pull up the standards generally and to encourage musicians such as Sybil Eaton and Imogen Holst, to help in the counties. She was enormously important in the RMSA and was able to persuade such musicians as Henry Wood, Hamilton Harty and Adrian Boult to support it.

Phyllis Ebsworth

Some of the Leading Conductors

Miss Ibberson told the Music Lovers' Club her views on some of the leading conductors whose methods she had studied and compared them with some of the continental conductors. She also

I was so glad to read Mark's article in 'The Friend'. This morning I was reading through an article I wrote about my first village class in the E. SA. bulletin of ? 1924. Following it was an article on 'Looking at Pictures' & signed Will Harvey These early days of E.S.A. were very happy & hopeful ones. Do you remember Edith & I coming up to Barmoor to practise? My love, & I wish you were nearer, Mary — Fieldfares. February 20th.

Note from Mary Ibberson to Mrs Margaret Harvey, undated, post-1953.

outlined her plans for the future development of the musical side of the Settlement's work. While in London Miss Ibberson had found time to learn a number of instruments and she gave demonstrations on some of them.

Letchworth Citizen (25 January 1929)

Quaker Harmony

Although Mary Ibberson was about to set up her own Rural Music School, taking with her many of the most talented musicians connected with the Settlement, the break appears to have been resolved in true Quaker harmony. For the next few years she still appeared on the Settlement's list of tutors, as did several of her colleagues, including Mrs Pryor and Mrs Elliott.

A Modest start

It had become clear to me that a comprehensive music service must, if it were to thrive, (a) have a separate existence, under the control of a musician; and (b) have its centre in a market town on which bus services converged, and which country people naturally visited. Letchworth was a wonderful place for people with ideas, but it was a newcomer and tended to be outside the normal life of the county; and it was in those days regarded with some suspicion. Nearby Hitchin was the market town for North Hertfordshire, well served by country buses and with a station on the main line from King's Cross. This seemed the ideal centre from which to make a start... We turned first to our old friends, the Thomas Wall Trustees, sending them particulars of a 'Proposal to form a rural music school in north Hertfordshire'... our application was warmly

supported by the warden of the Settlement, and the Trust promised a grant of £200 a year for three years and an additional £50 for equipment. Settlement friends and students most generously gave me an Austin 7 car and so it seemed possible to make a modest start in September.

Mary Ibberson (*For joy that we are here*)

The Hermitage

In 1929 the Seebohms' former home, the Hermitage was owned by John Ray, a builder and amateur musician. He made a small office available there for the new Hertfordshire Rural Music School with the address 86A, Bancroft, Hitchin. By 1930 as work expanded rapidly, the office space was increased and the address changed to 109, Bancroft. Meanwhile, Mary Ibberson herself needed somewhere to live. After her mother died in March 1929 she had left Letchworth and had been living in a cottage on the Pryors' estate at Weston. Fortunately it proved possible to adapt the Rural Music School's accommodation to incorporate a small flat and in the summer of 1930, Mary Ibberson moved in, accompanied by Edith Grubb, who was 'a wonderful housekeeper and cook, as well as an enthusiastic and experienced teacher and cellist, a keeper of the instruments and a wise adviser.'

Ethne Pryor

Ethne (pronounced 'Enna') Pryor was a talented artist and a keen musician, not a brilliant violinist, but enthusiastic. She played in the orchestra and probably helped *financially. She used to come over every Thursday to have a violin lesson with mother, brought by the chauffeur who then took both of them to the orchestra rehearsal at the old Music School in Bancroft. I used to come home from school [Hitchin Girls' Grammar School] with my satchel and sit on the steps and listen to the end of the rehearsal.*

Linnaea Walker (daughter of Phyllis Elliott)

Preliminary prospectus

The preliminary prospectus of the Hertfordshire Rural Music School, was issued in January 1930 and an advisory board was set up, consisting of: Adrian Boult, D.R. Burnet, Harvey Grace, Editha Knocker, Ernest Read, Geoffrey Shaw and Arthur Somervell. Sir Walford Davies was president, with D.J. Capper of the Rural Community Council as secretary, Hugh Seebohm as treasurer and Mary Ibberson as director. The first patrons were; Harry Plunket Greene, the singer, and Sir Walford Davies and within a year Colonel W.M. Pryor of Weston, Sir Henry Wood and the Countess of Strathmore, at St Paul's Waldenbury, all became patrons.

The Seebohms remembered

I remember the Seebohms very well. Hugh was our Chairman of Governors at school and Miss Esther took a great financial interest

Number 109, Bancroft. The entrance is between the white columns in the centre of the picture.

in the RMS and always came to concerts. She was grey haired, gentle, nice, rather small, and a perfect lady.

Linnaea Walker (daughter of Phyllis Elliott)

The Eyre Trio

Phyllis Elliott (née Eyre), was a professional musician who had studied under Joseph Joachim in Berlin. She and her sisters, Margery and Ruth performed in London concert halls as the Eyre Trio. She also taught the violin, at her home at the Plash, Bedwell Lane, Stevenage, where her pupils included a little girl by the name of Elizabeth Poston, who grew up to be a noted composer. Her contribution to the Rural Music School was invaluable: apart from the excellence of her playing, she brought the School closer to the world of professional music. When Hitchin's historian, Reginald Hine needed an expert opinion as to the authenticity of an iron fiddle, purporting to have belonged to John Bunyan, he naturally turned to Phyllis Elliott for advice.

Bunyan's Fiddle

Dear Mrs Elliott,

1. You were so helpful in reporting upon Bunyan's iron fiddle to my friend Percy Scholes that I should like you to have a reprint of my own article, in which your description is quoted in full.

2. Very many thanks to you for your interest…
3. I wish I could persuade J.B. [John Beagarie, of the Larches, Hitchin, who then owned the fiddle] to have it stringed and played upon by you, but he is afraid it would weaken or snap the rather fragile neck. I shall overcome that someday and then beseech you to give us a xviith century recital upon it.

Sincerely yours,
Reginald L. Hine

Letter to Phyllis Elliott (19 March 1934)

Some of the Founders

Mary Ibberson had a very authoritative manner. She had to do the conducting and organise the whole Music School. She was a charming, dark-haired person and she used to come over [to Stevenage] and play with Mother. Joyce Goodman lived in Chiltern Road, Hitchin. She was a great support to Mary Ibberson, a sweet person, a great friend of mother's. She had the 'earphone' hair style. So did mother until she was getting ready for a visit to America in 1932. Then she spent a day in London having her hair cut and permed. Katherine Tudor-Pole – known as T.P. – lived in Letchworth, a little person, she played the violin in the orchestra. So did Amy Purdy. Mrs Waldron Swann played the 'cello in the days when everyone was supposed to wear black for posh concerts. She hated black and always wore white. Occasionally I went with mother to see the three Miss Wrights, in their big house in Tilehouse Street, on the right going up. They played 'cello and violin.

Linnaea Walker (Phyllis Elliott's daughter)

A Splendid Team

In 1933 Hitchin Girls' Grammar School pupils were given a half-day holiday to celebrate the centenary of their founder, Frederic Seebohm. Mary Ibberson, in hospital after a motoring accident, was unable to help with final preparations for that year's Founders' Day Concert but the 'splendid team' headed by Gina Bacchus, Mercy Collisson and Joyce Goodman, with Editha Knocker conducting the instrumentalists, ensured that the event was a great success.

Violin lessons

Mrs Dorothy Berry, widow of Reginald, remembers the days when Miss Tudor-Pole used to go to the Berry family's house in Little Wymondley, to teach the double bass, and the Friday evenings when Joyce Goodman came to teach the violin. When Reginald and Dorothy were married, they walked under an arch of violins. Mary Ibberson started the Wymondley Choral Society in the British Legion Hall, coming every Monday to conduct. Mrs Berry thought she was 'A lovely lady with a lovely personality.' Wymondley also had its orchestra, which was trained by Mary Ibberson or Katherine Tudor-Pole. There were about fourteen players, all from Wymondley apart from one girl from Todds Green. The orchestra also had a social function, in that it provided an interest for young people in a small village and gave them opportunities to join with others.

Public Concerts

The activity at Wymondley was repeated in many villages throughout north

Chamber Music Group, February 1939.

Hertfordshire and beyond, including some parts of Bedfordshire. As the movement gained strength and the number of classes grew, public concerts become increasingly important in the lives of the students. Christmas Concerts in the Town Hall in the 1930s were unforgettable experiences for those who took part including Dorothy Berry and Linnaea Walker. The latter also has clear recollections of the Founders' Day Concerts, when she went with her mother to rehearse at the Hitchin Town Hall in the morning, then to the Pryors at Lannock Manor for lunch and back to the Town Hall for the concert in the afternoon. At the 1932 Founders' Day Concert, when Sir Adrian Boult conducted, she found him 'wonderful with children.'

Training the unmusical child – Is it worthwhile?

First, how is one to make sure he is unmusical? It seems to me the best plan, on first receiving a pupil, would be to have a friendly heart to heart talk with him, and ask him why he wants to learn... Then in a simple method give a test of ear, sense of rhythm and time.

Of course I realise this is more easily done with a private individual pupil, than when a batch of village children are starting.. Some will find that they are not invited to perform solos in the first fortnight, and so will drop out. These, and the proved unmusical ones would be better employed doing something they really have a gift for, and the teacher would be better employed working on promising material of which surely there is plenty. After all there is a limit to every teacher's vitality and patience, and by cutting out the hopeless ones he or she can give better value to promising pupils, and they in turn are not held back by the hopeless cases.

Phyllis Elliott (unpublished, undated manuscript)

A Federation of Rural Music Schools

Following swiftly on the example of Hertfordshire, other Rural Music Schools were being established until eventually in 1951 there were fifteen. As early as 1934 the first four Music Schools, Hertfordshire, Hampshire, Wiltshire and East Sussex, formed themselves into a federation, using the Hertfordshire Rural Music School office in Bancroft as their base. Dr George Dyson, Director of Music at Winchester College, was the first president and Mary Ibberson was released from some of her teaching duties 'in order to act as organiser and speaker as the occasion arose.' She was able to attend conferences, including the International Conference on Music Education, in Prague in April 1936 and to make many new contacts.

This photograph first appeared in For joy that we are here *(p. 47) and shows the Berry family of Little Wymondley. Walter (with double bass) and his wife Adeline and their sons, left to right, John, Reginald and Frank.*

Joyce Goodman (standing left) taking a chamber music class at 109, Bancroft, 1939.

Between 1935 and 1938 the constitution of the Rural Music Schools Federation was enlarged in order to include music schools sponsored by universities and other authorities, even those in urban areas. This more widely-based organization, renamed the Rural Music Schools Council, was then regarded by the Carnegie United Kingdom Trust as having national status and was thus eligible for larger grants under its policy. An immediate benefit was the appointment of Ronald Biggs, whose work in rural Devon was much admired by Mary Ibberson, as co-director, with her, of the Council.

It was becoming increasingly difficult to arrange meetings at locations convenient to representatives of all the far-flung strongholds of the Federation, in days when

the majority of people did not possess a motor car. Even in Hertfordshire, a geographically small county, it was impossible for students from west Hertfordshire to reach Hitchin in the north of the county by public transport and so the 1934 Founders' Day concert had to be held at Friends House in Euston Road, London. Even today it is a standing joke in the county that the best place to live if you want easy access to the whole of Hertfordshire is half-way between King's Cross and Euston.

Headquarters in London

The London office became absolutely necessary as the growth both of the Federation and of the

Hertfordshire Rural Music School made it impossible for me and the valiant Hertfordshire secretary to cope with the work... We were allowed the use of a large room for meetings [at the premises of the British Federation of Competition Festivals, 106, Gloucester Place, W.1]

Mary Ibberson (For joy that we are here)

BBC Broadcast

In November 1938, Ronald Biggs took a leading part in organizing the long-remembered concert in the Royal Albert Hall, in which amateur musicians from nine music schools across the country took part. An exciting element was the twenty-minute BBC broadcast of the programme, conducted by Adrian Boult, which included choral work from the first performance of 'In Windsor Forest' by Ralph Vaughan Williams. The whole event was a great success.

Official Journal

On 1 July 1934 the first issue of the Federation's official journal, *Rural Music* was published. It was a foolscap-sized publication and its contents included; Herbert J. Foss on 'Music in our Social Life'; Editha Knocker on 'Fiddle Technique'; Mary Ibberson on 'Rural Music Schools'; Sydney H. Lovett on 'Rural Church Music' and an interview with Sir Adrian Boult by Clemence Kerr. Initially printed free by the River Press in Salisbury, it failed to reach the desired circulation of one thousand and from issue number three it was edited by an editorial board chaired by Ethne Pryor and

printed by Letchworth Printers.Six more issues of *Rural Music* followed until, in the autumn of 1939, the Second World War put an end to that publication as to so much else.

CHAPTER 3

Rural Music Schools

Recorder class, Kimpton. (John Lea)

The Great and the Good

The first annual report of the Rural Music Schools Council was published for the year ending 31 July 1939. Its list of patrons and members reads like a roll-call of the musical establishment of the day. Patrons included: Sir Hugh Allen, Sir Adrian Boult, Dame Elizabeth Cadbury, Harold H. Child, Sir Walford Davies, Lady Montgomery Massingberd, Lady Mayer and Ernest Read.

Members representing Rural Music Schools were: Miss E. Burder and Miss Edwina Palmer (East Sussex) Lady Stephen and Miss Cicely Card (Hampshire) Mrs. Pryor and Miss Mary Ibberson (Hertfordshire) Mrs Slater and Miss Christine Godwin (Norfolk) Miss Plater and Miss Sybil Eaton (Wiltshire).

Members representing other bodies included: Miss Chambers (Head Mistresses' Association), T.E. Jones (Head Masters'

Association), Freda, Countess of Listowel (National Federation of Women's Institutes), Dr. R. Vaughan Williams (English Folk Dance and Song Society).

Dr George Dyson was President, Miss Editha Knocker, Chairman, Hugh E. Seebohm, Hon.Treasurer and Miss Mary Ibberson and Ronald Biggs were Directors.

With so many achievements already behind her and such an array of 'the great and the good' enlisted for the future, Mary Ibberson's progress and that of the movement she founded, seemed assured. There were now more than 2,000 students taking lessons in the five Rural Music Schools. But a month after this report was published, England was at war with Germany.

Editha Knocker's Birthday

When Editha Knocker was seventy, in 1939, there was a big birthday celebration at the Mayfair Hotel in London which marked the beginning of her fund to help the RMSA. Friends and students donated money for a present and she asked for it to be given to the RMSA. The Second World war was a terrible blow to her, cutting short her work in London and she went to live with Mrs Croll at her Scottish estate, Salaman Glenuig. She was not a public figure, but only known to important musicians of the time. Whenever we broadcast she wrote to say how much she had enjoyed it. That showed her continued interest in her pupils.

Phyllis Ebsworth

Travellers

It was anticipated that the Second World War would, at the very least, have an adverse effect on the work of the Rural Music Schools, but surprisingly, almost miraculously, they found themselves in greater demand than ever. The Council for the Encouragement of Music and the Arts (CEMA), was formed in 1940. It employed peripatetic music teachers, called Travellers who, for convenience, were attached to the central RMS Council. From their work the demand arose for an annual conference for Travellers and the directors of the various Rural Music Schools, an innovation which met with wide approval.

A Wider Audience Than Ever Before

One of the least expected happenings of the war was the great revival of interest in music. Hastily organised concerts in air-raid shelters, financed by CEMA, leading on to concerts in war factories and hostels, and the visits of London orchestras to the provinces, touched a wider audience than ever before; while at the same time CEMA travellers, inspired by Sir Walford Davies, were going out into the villages and encouraging amateurs to make music for themselves.

Mary Ibberson (Making Music, May 1946)

Training Courses at Hitchin

The evacuation of the BBC Symphony Orchestra from London to Bedford had the effect of stimulating Bedfordshire to establish its own Rural Music School in 1940. Previously it had been affiliated to the Hertfordshire School. Another, even more exciting development in the same year, was the provision of grants from the Carnegie

United Kingdom Trust to enable the RMSC to provide training courses at its Hitchin office for a small number of qualified musicians who would go on to take up teaching work in rural areas. The first of these was Grisell Roy.

Music on a Motor Bike

I came to the Hertfordshire Rural Music School in the autumn of 1941. I wrote to Mary Ibberson when I had to leave my school job. She was able to obtain funds from Eric Walter White of the Community Council for me to 'experience the peculiar milieu of a Rural Music School' as a student for three months and then they kept me on the staff and paid me a graduate teacher's salary, about £200 per year. I worked in the office, taught choral societies such as Welwyn Garden City and Dunstable, and history of music courses for the Workers' Educational Association, and I visited Women's Institute meetings for sessions of community singing at £1 a time.

After a time Hertfordshire County Council gave the Rural Music School a grant to organise singing festivals and concerts for primary schools and I bought myself a motorbike. At conferences I met people running some of the other music schools, doing the same sort of job as Mary Ibberson. The various Rural Music Schools later combined to form the Rural Music Schools' Association. Mercy Collisson was running Bedfordshire RMS and Gina Bacchus was working in West Herts then, at Tring. The idea was that people living in villages, whether children or adults, had no access to instrumental music lessons and couldn't afford them anyway – so by teaching a class you could make it possible economically – just.

Grisell Davies (nee Roy)

A Gift to the Girls' Grammar School

Esther Seebohm had lived alone at Little Benslow Hills, apart from her domestic staff, since her sister Hilda's death in 1931. She continued to take a great interest in the Rural Music Schools movement and in Hitchin Girls' Grammar School, with which her family had been so intimately connected. In 1927 she gave the school a strip of land, with the small wood that has given so much pleasure to generations of pupils and teachers. In appreciation, and apparently quite spontaneously, all the girls at the school in 1941 contributed to a cheque which they gave to Miss Seebohm at Christmas, for any good cause she chose. Accompanying the cheque was a poem by a pupil, Mary Holliday, which ended;

'Although the world outside may never know
Your kindness, yet the little world of School
Will not forget.'

Written at Little Benslow Hills

Your beautiful flowers, the gold and white Chrysanthemums, are beside me on my table as I write and my father's portrait looks down on them and me. I want to thank you all in his name, as well as my own, for being so good to me. It would please him so much that we should be friends…

With the flowers and the cheque came, to crown all, that amazingly kind poem that quite took my breath away when I read it. I do thank you from my heart. It was such a kind thought that prompted you to take the trouble to assure me that we belong to one another as indeed I feel we do. It is a great pleasure to me to think of you roaming in the wood in your spare minutes, watching the rooks and their amusing ways and greeting the aconites when they come up as we used to do in days gone by...

Esther Seebohm, letter to Hitchin Girls' Grammar School, Christmas 1941

Gardener to the Seebohms

I have known Little Benslow Hills as long as I can remember. My grandfather, Arthur Barker, was head gardener to Miss Seebohm and my grandparents lived in the Lodge. Before and during the war my mother and I visited them on Saturdays. This of course was long before Ibberson Way existed, and there was a big grey gate across the entrance to the private road. The estate then, about twelve acres, was much larger than it is now, with wild-flower meadows and spinneys. I explored everywhere, except for the lawn and garden in front of the house. There was a range of greenhouses along the wall behind the water-tower, and I helped my grandfather with the watering.

Arthur Barker was born in 1865, and from 1890 he worked for Frederic Seebohm at the Hermitage. When Miss Esther and Miss Hilda purchased Benslow in 1925, Barker, as he was known, was sent ahead some months before the sisters moved, to 'get the place ready for them'. Miss Hilda had died in 1931, but she was still spoken of at the Lodge, as was another of the sisters, Lady Godlee (Juliet Seebohm, who had married Sir Rickman Godlee, physician to royalty). I heard this name as 'Lady Godly', and supposed her to be some important religious personage.

Miss Seebohm and I were acquainted, but to a small boy, the grandson of the gardener, she was a very grand lady. She sent to me, via my grandfather, interesting things: books of watercolours painted by her and her sisters when they were young, sixty years before; an album containing flowers from Bethlehem, and Victorian postage stamps torn from old envelopes. Sixty years later I still have these things.

My grandmother, Sarah Barker, died in 1938 when I was eight. Two years later, when my grandfather had worked for the Seebohms for fifty years, Miss Esther marked the occasion by gathering a bunch of flowers that he had grown and presenting them to him. He worked until the day he died, aged eighty-three, in 1948. He had to, because the Lodge was a tied cottage, and if he stopped working he would have had to leave.

Richard Wiggs

A Night with the Rector of Dunstable

I was sometimes allowed by Mary Ibberson to use her car to get to classes, which meant driving in the blackout with the very dim headlights which were permitted. (I also remember being ticked off by her for using it for some other purpose!) I used to take my bicycle by train to Welwyn North and ride to Tewin for the village choir rehearsals, spending the night there with Mr and Mrs Crowley. My earnings from these activities were paid to the RMS and contributed towards my salary. I went to Ivinghoe once to take a choir and stayed the night with the Rector of Dunstable. It was an old house – the bath had been put in a bedroom. I did something awful and flooded the house. Another time I had to entertain some Landgirls. We sang some songs and then came The Londonderry Air at which point one burst into tears!

Grisell Davies (nee Roy)

Miss Gina Bacchus with pupils at Ivinghoe village children's class. (John Lea)

Wartime in Wiltshire

During the 'invasion' year of the war, children in Bradford-on-Avon where I taught French, were allowed into school during the summer holidays and I gave musical appreciation sessions to entertain those children who turned up. The headmaster liked this and put it on my timetable for the VIth form, later adding ordinary music lessons for one class. It was at this point that I sought help from the Rural Music School directed by Christopher le Fleming and based in Tonbridge where I lived. Later I helped the RMSA in various ways and was elected to the council of the Wiltshire Rural Music School.

Doris Gare

Norman Hearn at Bermondsey

Norman Hearn and his wife Margaret had started, in association with a Methodist church, a centre for music in Bermondsey on RMS lines. He was very successful in attracting young people. The centre was affiliated to us and became a demonstration centre in East London. A number of students from the Royal Schools of Music were glad to help and to gain experience of work in the associated clubs and settlements.

Mary Ibberson (For joy that we are here)

Silent Prayer

The war impinged upon us very little – I had to firewatch in Bancroft. Mary Ibberson asked me if I wanted to register as a Conscientious Objector. I said, 'No' because I hadn't got the conviction, but I didn't want to be conscripted, I didn't want to leave this life. But I was not called up presumably because I was doing educational work for Hertfordshire County Council. In the Music School, always as a matter of routine at the beginning of the day there was a few minutes of silent prayer and whoever was there was invited to join. Helen Wright, secretary of the RMSA, didn't. Mary Ibberson was a heroine of mine, a great influence. This was her life, she regarded it as a mission. She was a mystic, I think – very kind and understanding. I learned a tremendous lot from her about religion and life. It was part of my growing-up period and discovering oneself as a person. She was very efficient. But I remember once, at a sort of conference at Offley, Helen Wright seemed to find her a little too intense.

Grisell Davies (nee Roy)

The Rural Music Schools Association

By the time the war ended in 1945, it had become clear that training teachers in all subjects was to be a priority in a country which desperately needed to rebuild homes, towns and cities and to restore disrupted lives. The 1944 Education Act had promised not only 'Secondary education for all' but also a broader framework of education, one that included music and the arts. The Rural Music Schools now found themselves in the forefront of the new plans for music education. Various forms of co-operation between the local education authorities and voluntary bodies were taking shape all over the country, as the county councils began setting up the nationwide provision of musical education.

Mary Ibberson noted approvingly that local authorities were now giving financial support to some of the Rural Music Schools, in return for their help and expertise. In 1946 the Rural Music Schools Federation became the Rural Music Schools Association (RMSA), a non-profit-making company. Its response to the shortage of trained music teachers was to set up 'a training centre in Hitchin, where teachers who have already passed through one of the Royal Schools, or some equivalent course, can obtain the extra training.'

We Got the Giggles

I had trained from 1942 to 1944 as an Infant/Nursery teacher at Homerton College, Cambridge. It was very much a 'no frills' course and although music teaching was to be an integral part of my work, I did not regard myself as a music teacher. I taught for two years in West Sussex (classes of forty pupils, for all subjects), where I met Edwina Palmer and Agnes Best – superb teachers and directors of Sussex Rural Music School in Lewes. Through them I heard about the training course at Hitchin and, having saved a little money and having been awarded a grant of £10 per term, by West Sussex County Council, I gave up my job and arrived in Hitchin in the autumn of 1946 as one of two students on the first training course. We had some excellent visiting teachers, including Imogen Holst and Watkins Shaw. We had Arthur Trew for 'cello lessons and Denis Brain, the horn-player, took part in the 'Messiah' – he gave me a wink. I played in the small orchestra and learnt the elements of conducting, which stood me in good stead. I also had to learn the recorder from Edith Grubb.

There were only two of us in the class and we got the giggles very easily.

Elizabeth Black (nee Mason)

A Grand lady

Mary Ibberson was a rather grand lady. I remember her very well. My mother was a very keen member of the choir in 1930s and throughout the war. I remember I attended a performance by Helen Wright, Mary Ibberson and Stephen Wilkinson. I was a violin student of Agnes Best in Sussex from 1951 to 1953. Later in the 1950s, when I had moved back to Letchworth I was a student of Romilly John (son of Augustus John) on the classical guitar. He came every fortnight to the office in the old Hermitage building. I last saw Mary Ibberson in the early 1950s.

Richard Wiggs

Post-War Reconstruction

The years immediately following the end of the war were full of activity and optimism. In June 1945, Sybil Eaton introduced Mary Ibberson to John and Jean Maud (later Lord and Lady Redcliffe-Maud) and the latter agreed to join the RMSA Council, of which she became chairman in 1949. The same year Imogen Holst invited Mary Ibberson and colleagues to teach at a Dartington summer school for a 'most memorable fortnight... Agnes Best coached pianists on keyboard improvisation... Here for the first time Gertrude Collins shared the violin class method lessons with Edwina Palmer.' At the end of 1945 the RMSA was able to re-open its London office. Finally and of most far-reaching importance, Esther Seebohm had offered Mary Ibberson some rooms at Little Benslow Hills during her lifetime, and to leave the whole property, including the grounds, for the use of the RMSA on her death.

Lots of ghosts

In 1946 Little Benslow Hills was dark and creepy. There were lots of ghosts and great trees, it was dark. There were only two of us here in my year, Muriel Anthony and I. She left after about one term. There was terrible snow. Agnes Best and Edwina Palmer couldn't get here from Sussex so I did some of the teaching. As ever money was a problem. They found me digs in Old Hale Way, they were cheap and I went everywhere on my bike.

Elizabeth Black (nee Mason)

Music lecturer at Balls Park

The local authority in Hertfordshire got very interested in us when they appointed their first Music Organiser – the idea of music classes in schools must have been helped by the RMS. I left Hitchin around 1946, when I went to Dartington where I was offered a three month course which became six months, under Imogen Holst. From there, on the suggestion of the Hertfordshire County Music Adviser, Harold Watkins Shaw, I applied for the post of Music Lecturer at their new Balls Park Training College for (primary) teachers, in Hertford. I had no primary teaching experience so I had to spend some time in primary schools to get it. I lived with my mother in Walkern Hall.

Grisell Davies (nee Roy)

Music Was Her Mission

Mary Ibberson had very penetrating eyes, rather forbidding. She said, 'These people have got to go away feeling better for the music. They have not had your privileges. It is your job to enable, encourage them.' Mary Ibberson was getting rural music schools set up in various places. She really was incredible, but fearsome. She was always addressed as Miss Ibberson. Music was her mission – music gets through and speaks to everyone. She would be so delighted that they have concerts in churches and everyone mixes. She loved people, liked meeting people, but she knew exactly what she was doing – she won people. She had an eye to business. She was keen to enable people.

Elizabeth Black (nee Mason)

First issue of 'Making Music'

Rural Music was the official journal of the Federation of Rural Music Schools. It was eagerly read and very much appreciated... Since the last issue... appeared in the autumn of 1939, an old world has vanished, and out of the present travail will surely emerge a new and better way of living, this time for the many, not merely for the few... And now the night has passed, and the cold clear light of morning calls us to work. Here is Making Music and, with it, greeting from the Rural Music Schools Association to its many friends, both old and new. A pause here to remember also those friends of our early days no longer with us. With thankful hearts we go forward, inspired by what they have done, determined to make the future such as they would think worthy of them, and of the best in us. The 'Interval' has been long. It is time to raise the curtain on Act II.

Christopher le Fleming, Editor, Making Music Number 1, May 1946.

Young Men from the Services

The secretarial and organisational aspect was good. I learned I had to get there in time to prepare the room for the orchestra and also how to look after the music and the instruments, the mechanics of it all. Mary Ibberson was very good at organization and preparation. This helped her to attract young men coming out of the services who were used to discipline. Quakers like things to be good but simple, they have high standards of discipline. A lot more men came into the Rural Music Schools after World War II. I got my ARCM in December 1948 and went to Wiltshire in 1949 under Michael Vickers, who was Rural Music School Director and County Music Adviser all in one – very efficient. Michael Vickers had come out of the army. We cycled round to the villages and little children paid their shillings – they were sweet.

Elizabeth Black (nee Mason)

Death of Hugh Seebohm, 16 July 1946

The centre of the Hertfordshire Music School is in the old home of the Seebohm family in Hitchin, and our first music room was the room in which Hugh Seebohm was born. From the day he consented to be Treasurer until his death he took the keenest interest in all that went on and gave us his personal service, whether it was interviewing the Ministry of Education, playing with the orchestra on Founders' Day or giving a lucid explanation of a balance sheet at an Annual Meeting. A week or two before his death I went to see him, on the Hertfordshire Founders' Day – the first he had missed. I told him we should be thinking of him. He smiled and said: 'Don't make too much of me.'

Mary Ibberson, in Making Music Number 2, October 1946

Help from Aldeburgh

Hugh Seebohm's son, George, took over as treasurer. His daughter Fidelity, who was married to the Earl of Cranbrook, had been for many years chairman of the Aldeburgh Festival Committee and it was with her

Founders' Day, Hitchin, 1951. Left to right, Norman Fulton, Mary Ibberson, Stephen Wilkinson.

encouragement that Ursula Nettleship, Benjamin Britten and Peter Pears offered to help with an ambitious RMSA Festival Concert being planned and organised by Christopher le Fleming.

Festival Concert in Southwark Cathedral

The Court Circular issued on June 25th, 1949, contained the following item: 'Queen Mary, accompanied by the Earl of Harewood and attended by the Lady Constance Milnes Gaskell and Captain the Lord Claud Hamilton, was present at a Festival Concert held under the auspices of the Rural Music Schools Association in Southwark Cathedral this evening'. The concert was organised by the RMSA with the expert and invaluable assistance of the Imperial Concert Agency. The object was to give some music in London in connection with the appeal and publicity side of RMSA activities. The chance of giving the first London performance of Benjamin Britten's cantata 'St Nicolas' was not to be missed... The composer and Peter Pears most generously gave their services.

Report in Making Music Number 11, Autumn 1949

A New Director

In 1947 Sir George Dyson resigned as president after thirteen years and Lord Harewood 'consented to take his place.' In that same year Mary Ibberson herself resigned the directorship of the Hertfordshire Rural Music School because 'The school was expanding and so was the RMSA and both needed full-time directors. Stephen Wilkinson, well-known now as the

Rehearsing for the 21st Anniversary Concert, Royal Albert Hall, November 1950.

conductor of the Northern Singers, was appointed as my successor. '

Closing of a chapter

As the last Hallelujah of Purcell's Evening Hymn died away in the warm air of a June night, a vigorous little woman flicked away her baton, waved a hand at singers and orchestra, and turned to acknowledge the applause of the large audience in Hitchin Town Hall. It was the culmination of an ambition, the last personal episode in a musical dream come true.

When Miss Mary Ibberson stepped down

from the rostrum to receive the handshakes of friends, it was more than the end of another Hertfordshire Rural Music School Founders' Day concert. It was the closing of a chapter in the history of the whole Rural Music School movement, for it was Miss Ibberson's last appearance as director at Hitchin... Mrs E. Pryor, a member of the Board of Governors, reminded them that they could not be sad at Miss Ibberson's departure, for it was given to few people to see their ideas grow to such fruition. She had launched the project at the beginning, and had carried it on herself.

Miss Ibberson... rose to thank Hitchin for the help she had received in the early days. It was a matter of great satisfaction, she said,

39

that the heart of the movement would stay in Hitchin, for she recalled the welcome it had received there originally. 'Hitchin people did not look at us askance, as they might have done,' she said. 'They made us feel very much at home.'

Hertfordshire Pictorial newspaper,
1 July 1947

Successor to Miss Ibberson

Mr Stephen Wilkinson possesses all the attributes of a successor to Miss Ibberson, whose enthusiasm has been the principal factor in building up the movement... An

Ralph Vaughan Williams, 13 April 1949. (Courtesy BBC)

MA of Cambridge University, he was studying there when war broke out. He joined the Navy, and was de-mobbed after five years on active service, and returned to Cambridge to complete his studies, and obtained his degree of Bachelor of Music. This is his first appointment, and he takes over on September 1st. His youth and training combined should equip him for an appointment of interest and unique artistic opportunity.

Hertfordshire Pictorial newspaper,
1 July 1947

Twenty-first Anniversary Concert

In 1950 the Rural Music Schools' Association celebrated its twenty-first anniversary year. A fitting celebration was called for, something that would allow as many representatives as possible, from all the Rural Music Schools, to take part. With some trepidation, it was decided to book the Royal Albert Hall. Sir Adrian Boult agreed to conduct and Ralph Vaughan Williams composed his Concerto Grosso for string orchestra especially for the occasion. There were months of preparation before the great day, Saturday 18 November 1950, but when it arrived, the concert was an outstanding success, made even more special by the presence of Queen Elizabeth (now the Queen Mother). This was the occasion of Sir Steuart Wilson's oft-quoted speech, in which he said, 'If Your Majesty were to start from your home at Sandringham to walk to Plymouth Hoe, you would not go far without an opportunity to pick up a music lesson on the way.'

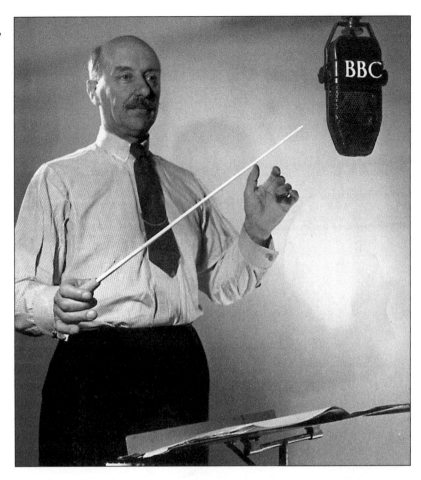

*Sir Adrian Boult,
11 April 1947.
(Courtesy BBC)*

Sadly, 1950 was also the year in which the RMSA lost two of its greatest friends. On 19 September, Editha Knocker died. Apart from her great gifts as a player, conductor and teacher, she had contributed to music education in practical ways, setting up the Violin Loan Scheme in 1932 and giving the money which friends and admirers collected for her seventieth birthday in 1939, to help the RMSA. Following her death, this gift became the basis of a memorial fund in her name. The Editha Knocker memorial Fund was enormously successful, supported by such people as Sybil Eaton, the Griller Quartet, Benjamin Britten and Peter Pears, all of whom gave concerts for it. Her contribution was such, Mary Ibberson declared, that the whole of the RMSA should be a monument to her.

As a coda to the year, Esther Seebohm died in December, aged ninety.

CHAPTER 4

To be Held on Trust

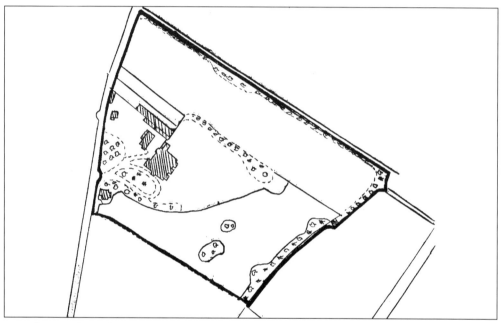

Map showing the Little Benslow Hills estate as left to the Rural Music Schools Association in 1951.

Bequest to the RMSA

Apart from a piece of land which she wished conveyed to the Hitchin Urban District Council, Esther Seebohm left the Little Benslow Hills estate for the use of the RMSA. She did not include an endowment for its upkeep, although previously she had given monetary donations to the RMSA, and Council had known for some years that she intended leaving them the house and gardens.

The Will

... 4. I devise (free of death and other duties) my messuage gardener's cottage and the buildings thereto belonging known as 'Little Benslow Hills' together with such part of the garden and lands thereto belonging as are for the purposes of identification delineated and edged red on the plan...

... 5. I declare that if the Rural Music Schools Association accept the devise contained in clause 4 hereof the said property shall be held by

them upon trust to use the same or permit the same to be used for the advancement of musical education in rural areas in such manner as the said Rural Music Schools Association shall from time to time determine and I declare that for this purpose the said Rural Music Schools Association may use the whole or any part of the same as a headquarters or as a training centre upon such terms or conditions as the said Rural Music Schools Association shall think fit and I further declare that in the event of the said Rural Music Schools Association being through any cause unable at any time to administer the charitable trusts hereinbefore declared the said Rural Music Schools Association shall by deed appoint some other corporation or person or persons to be a trustee or trustees thereof in its place and I further declare that except where precluded by the context the Rural Music Schools Association shall include the trustee or trustees for the time being of the charitable trusts hereinbefore declared...

'At Home' at Little Benslow Hills, 1950s.

Extract from Esther Seebohm's will

The Legacy

On Saturday 19 January, 1952, Mary Ibberson, her solicitor, James Lindsell and the RMSA Treasurer, Matthew Pryor, met to discuss the implications of accepting the bequest. The minutes of that meeting record, 'The treasurer asked whether, if it became later on impossible for financial or other reasons to use Little Benslow Hills for the purposes of the Trust, the Association would be free to sell it. Mr Lindsell said they would, provided the proceeds of the sale were devoted to the purposes of the Trust.' In May 1952, Little Benslow Hills became the property of the RMSA.

In the wake of the 1944 Education Act, local education authorities were beginning to take over the teaching of music in rural areas. While this was a compliment to the RMSA, a confirmation of its success, at the same time it placed a question mark over its future role. The legacy of Little Benslow Hills could be seen as providential, as it offered the opportunity of shifting the emphasis towards residential courses and work with adults, but at the same time, the prospect of taking responsibility for the staffing and maintenance of the property was daunting. The problem would lie in getting the financial and management structures right.

Meanwhile, the RMSA's London office was closed in 1952 and Little Benslow Hills became its headquarters. The same year, with a view to at least partial retirement, Mary Ibberson asked the RMSA Council if she might build a bungalow in the grounds and was given permission. She named the bungalow 'Fieldfares', a nice confusion of the former name for William Ransom's house, 'Fairfield.'

Hard Work, But Enjoyable

I went to Benslow in 1951 to help in the house. Miss Esther Seebohm was there for nearly a year after I came. People told me that she was austere, but I knew her as an old, old, lady and she was very sweet. She had a housekeeper and two maids. Then I worked in

Jack and Eileen Maylin, July 1975.

the garden. I was a farmer's daughter, so I knew about outdoor work. When Brian Shepherd left, my husband and I moved into the Lodge and did gardening and maintenance work between us. It was very hard work but I enjoyed it very much, particularly when Mary Ibberson was there. Then Helen Wright, took over and she was a very nice person too, like Miss Ibberson. She was very clever, she had lived in Italy for a time and she spoke nine languages.

Eileen Maylin

Holst's Music

In 1951 I came to teach in Letchworth as Head of Languages at Letchworth Grammar School. I had really forgotten about the Rural Music Schools Association by that time, although I had been involved in different sorts of music at Southend. I attended day courses organised by Mary Ibberson. David Willcocks gave a whole day and Stephen Wilkinson came and did a day in Miss Ibberson's time. Imogen Holst came and conducted for a day, bringing a lot of her father's music. It had not been published and she wanted to sort it out, so we sang it for her. Mary Ibberson ran the day, with Imogen Holst conducting. There were courses for instrumentalists as well.

Doris Gare

The Gardens Were Beautiful

There were about six acres of gardens and they were absolutely beautiful. There was the walled garden with grapes and figs. We had the field at that time, with a tulip tree and a wych elm. They were cut down, by mistake it was said. When I first went, there was another field below the Lodge, where the school has been built, off Benslow Lane. Mary Ibberson was a keen gardener too. She had a beautiful garden at Fieldfares, about a quarter of an acre. It was built about 1952, after I came. Before that she lived in the house, in what is now the Ibberson room. I knew Miss Grubb too. She was very nice, very tall and upright, very fair to everyone. They had a cat called Julie, because it arrived in July. It was a stray and kept getting in the garage and sleeping in the car. In the end they kept it.

Eileen Maylin

Immense Personal Authority

Mary Ibberson – Oh, she was lovely. Unassuming, very quiet, of immense personal authority. Lady Redcliffe-Maud was also a formidable person and let you know it, but Mary never did, you had to find it out for yourself. She was not just a Quaker – she was very much a Quaker. After one of the meetings we had tea in her bungalow. She was always very charming and very pleasant to meet.

Francis Oakes

Plaque Unveiled

On 20 July 1953, the bronze plaque commemorating Editha Knocker, was unveiled at Little Benslow Hills, by Mrs Croll and Basil Cameron.

Loyal and Happy Comradeship

Hertfordshire [Rural Music School]: *Our Director, Stephen Wilkinson, left us on*

Rural Music Schools Association

President:
THE RT. HON. THE EARL OF HAREWOOD
Vice-President:
DR. REGINALD JACQUES
Chairman of Council:
LADY MAUD

Programme

for the

OPENING OF THE ASSOCIATION'S CENTRE

LITTLE BENSLOW HILLS
HITCHIN

on

Saturday, July 18th, 1953

This Programme Admits Bearer

Programme for the opening of Rural Music Schools Association's Centre at Little Benslow Hills, 1953.

November 28th 1953 to take a post with the BBC in Leeds. He carries with him our good wishes for his future career. During the past six and a half years his fine musicianship has raised continuously the standard of the School and his stimulating personality has bound its members into a particularly loyal and happy comradeship. At a farewell party we were able to express our appreciation in words and in the presentation of a brief-case, cheque and book of signatures of subscribers. We hope to welcome our new Director, Mr Evelyn Webb, in March.

Making Music, Number 24, Spring 1954

The Silver Jubilee Concert

The twenty-fifth anniversary of the foundation of the Rural Music Schools was celebrated in a blaze of splendour in Southwark Cathedral on January 30th, 1954. The 'Music for Candlemas' brought a shining warmth to a grey and snowy afternoon, reflecting the transition from darkness to light in the Christian year, and conveying also the miraculous increase of strength in the life of the Rural Music Schools.

The outstanding event of the programme was the performance of Lennox Berkeley's Stabat Mater which was deeply impressive... Bach's Cantata No. 118 opened the Jubilee year with a triumphant burst of glory; the Pastoral Cantata of Alessandro Scarlatti, where Margaret Ritchie's voice floated up to the roof in effortless grace; and Vaughan William's Benedicite, where the Rural Music Schools choir and the orchestra, under Dr Paul Steinitz, achieved a balance between calm assurance and boundless enthusiasm. This is the balance that all music makers are perpetually trying to reach: there can be no doubt that they come nearest to it when amateurs and professionals are able to work together as they do in the Rural Music Schools Association.

Imogen Holst, Making Music, Number 24, Spring 1954

Christmas Concert 1957. Left to right, -?-, Olive Skells, Vera Charlwood, Evelyn Webb. (Courtesy Herts. Pictorial)

Garden Party, 10 July 1954.

Mary Ibberson's OBE

The Spring, 1955, issue of *Making Music* carried the brief announcement that Miss Mary Ibberson had been awarded the OBE in the New Year Honours, 'for services to music.'

She Shared Her Love of Music

I did not know Mary Ibberson well. She appeared to be a quiet, gentle, purposeful lady. She was always welcoming, never inquisitive yet quickly aware of individual needs. She shared her love of music and increased people's expectation of achievement. She always wanted to hear what we had accomplished at the end of a course.

Ruth Maguire

News from RMSA Headquarters

Concerts in aid of the Editha Knocker Fund for the Rural Music Schools were given by Margaret Ritchie (at Little Benslow Hills), and by Sybil Eaton, Daphne Ibbott and Audrey Strange (in Ash church, near Canterbury), in June. All these artists generously gave their services.

The annual Summer School for String Teachers at Roehampton attracted a larger number than ever before, the house being full to capacity; and the Music Holiday Week at Offley also had its full complement of amateurs.

The RMSA centre at Little Benslow Hills was extensively used throughout the summer. The house was used for weekends by the Bedford and District Holiday Fellowship (Ramblers' Group), the St Andrews University Madrigal Group; and the Cambridge Technical

College Opera Group; and for shorter periods by the Hertfordshire Rural Music School for the annual fete organised by their students' association, and by the Associated Board for their local examinations. Various individuals have stayed in the house for periods varying from a week to two months, looking after themselves and enjoying the chance of uninterrupted practice.

Making Music, Number 29, Autumn 1955

Continually Rising Costs

Events at Little Benslow Hills have included a day for recorder players and one for choral singers, and weekends for listeners and for chamber music players. The number of individual bookings has been greater than usual for the time of year. Meetings of the 'Neighbourhood Music Circle' and the Hitchin Gramophone Club have taken

Arthur Trew, October 1960.

place regularly. The house was used for two days in December for the Associated Board examinations; and in October for a conference of Rural Music School Directors. The staff organised a Christmas Party in aid of Hungarian relief which raised about £16.

Much time has been spent during the autumn and winter in visits to Rural Music Schools for consultations with their officers and with Education Authorities. It is a matter of real concern to all how the work is going to be financed in the future, with continually rising costs, particularly in Burnham Scale salaries. It is hoped that it will be possible to reach some agreement with Education Authorities whereby a balance can be maintained between security and freedom. This was also the main theme of the Association's Ordinary General Meeting in December, which was held by kind invitation at the house of Lady Maud, chairman of the Council. Lord Harewood presided. Reports were given by the Treasurer, the Director, and by two of the Schools' Directors (Miss Cholmeley, Suffolk and Mr Mills, Bedfordshire). From these it emerged that the following subjects are now being taught, to adults and children in Rural Music Schools: piano, campanology, recorder, clarinet, oboe, flute, all brass, musicianship, theory, harmony, choral and solo singing, and all stringed instruments, including the Spanish guitar. Those who persist in thinking that Rural Music Schools deal only in children's violin classes, please note!

Making Music, Number 33, Spring 1957

A Wonderful Collection of Books

I first went to Little Benslow Hills in the late 1950s or early '60s. Mary Ibberson had 'phoned Hitchin Library, where I was Branch Librarian, and asked if someone could go up to

Edwina Palmer giving a violin class demonstration at the UNESCO Conference, Brussels, July 1953.

Little Benslow Hills to advise on cataloguing all her books. As soon as I went through the front door, the thing that struck me was the wallpaper. It had a beautiful wildflower pattern, which seemed right for a rural music school. I was shown into a large room on the ground floor and there were books everywhere, on the shelves, piled up on the floor and Mary Ibberson was sitting in the middle of them. It was a wonderful collection of books and Mary Ibberson was very anxious to get it organised. We had a long discussion and I left some ideas with her and came back about a month later for another talk.

Kay Petrie

Farewell to 109, Bancroft

As local education authorities throughout the country took increasing responsibility for music education, so the role of the RMSA diminished. In Hertfordshire, the County Council, which had helped support the Rural Music School for many years, decided to take complete control from 1 April 1958. Even so, it would not be able to maintain the status quo, but announced that the post of Director would be 'put into temporary abeyance for reasons of economy' and Eric Bimrose, the County Music Organiser, would take over supervision of the School. On 25 July 1959, the Hertfordshire Rural Music School moved from its home of thirty years, at 109, Bancroft, to Highbury House. This building had for many years been the boarding house of Hitchin Girls' Grammar School and, until the last boarders left in 1960, the premises would be shared with them. Interestingly, the Rural Music School would still be on Quaker territory, as Highbury

House was originally the home of Benjamin Seebohm. Other changes were taking place, as Mary Ibberson retired from full-time work on 1st October 1959. She continued as part-time Director of the RMSA. Bernard Shore, recently retired from the post of Chief Inspector in Music to the Minister of Education, worked with her, also on a part-time basis. Miss Helen Wright became Assistant Director.

First Visit

My first visit to Little Benslow Hills was in the late '50s, to a small string group led by Bernard Shore. There were still residents on the top floor, from war-time. The first floor rooms were dormitories. Library shelves clad the walls of the landing at the top of the first stairway. The present dining room was the only music room/lounge, with two grand pianos. The present bar was the office, the present Macnaghten Room was the dining room, with a huge table round which the Cadbury firm had had their meetings in war-time.

Ruth Maguire

Running the Estate

The rights and responsibilities of running Benslow swiftly made themselves apparent,

A string course in Bedford, 1954, Bernard Shore conducting. (Courtesy Bedford Times and Citizen)

Chamber Music Day, Little Benslow Hills, October 1954. (Gordon Coombes Ltd)

as the national surge in the building of new houses, schools and roads boosted the demand for land and local authorities and development corporations were given powers of compulsory purchase in certain circumstances. In this new, land-hungry world, it was not surprising that individuals and organisations sometimes took the opportunity for short-term gain.

Meadows and Spinneys Bulldozed Away

When Miss Esther died in 1951, placing Benslow in trust for the use of the RMSA, she bequeathed to the town the two meadows and the spinneys on the hillside below the house, 'as a Garden or Open Space to which the residents of Hitchin may resort as a place of rest and quietude...' But before long the

A corner of the hall, Little Benslow Hills, 1950s. (Ursula Hartleben)

meadows and spinneys were bulldozed away and the site was filled with the 'bricks and mortar' and tarmac of St Andrew's School.

Richard Wiggs

The Value of Land

Having been advised that its land would be worth more if it carried outline planning permission for residential building, the RMSA applied to the Hitchin Urban District Council, causing some alarm. The UDC Surveyor replied on 29 January 1958, 'I have discussed the proposal with the Divisional Planning Officer and we both feel that the extremely attractive amenities of this area should be carefully preserved...' However, it appears that outline planning permission 'for their own possible future use' was eventually granted which, the RMSA felt, would enable it to ask 'the whole building price' if, as seemed possible, the question of compulsory purchase arose.

The RMSA's solicitor advised Helen Wright, on 23 November 1959, that 'the Association are now sitting on a gold-mine, as building land is now so short in Hitchin. You would have no difficulty in getting £2,000 or more per acre. I am not advising you to sell but just letting you know the extent to which the value of building land has risen in the last year'.

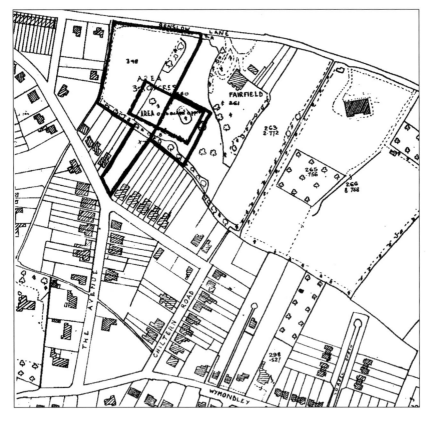

Little Benslow Hills estate in April 1952 (map copied from 1923 Ordnance Survey, still using the name 'Fairfield'). The land heavily outlined was subsequently sold.

The School Playing Field

In 1961, the anticipated request came from Hertfordshire County Council, asking the RMSA to sell approximately one acre of land to provide a football pitch for St Andrew's School next door. The RMSA was firmly against this, convinced that 'the sale of any part of the property would detract seriously from the amenities, and would also greatly diminish the value of the property as a whole should it ever be decided to sell it for development purposes.'

Retirement of Mary Ibberson

In 1962, at the age of seventy, Mary Ibberson retired, though she continued to live at Fieldfares. A concert was given in her honour at the Royal College of Music.

The post of Director of the RMSA passed to Helen Wright, who had been at the centre of RMSA administration for many years. She continued the correspondence with Hitchin UDC, reasserting that the the RMSA remained opposed to any sale, and she seems to have been personally committed to keeping the Little Benslow Hills land intact. However, on 27 February 1963, following a compulsory purchase order, she wrote to the RMSA Treasurer, Matthew Pryor, 'This, I suppose, is IT. Is there any chance you can come to the Council meeting on March 5th and help us in our deliberations? I imagine there is nothing more we can do but get as much money out of them as possible. I dislike the whole thing intensely... H.W.'

Country House Courses

My next contact was through Murray Gordon. A

singer and bass-player, he was by profession a Fleet Street journalist dealing with arts news. He organised a number of small courses, mainly singing, in country houses. Mary Ibberson was interested and invited him to hire Benslow, in an attempt to make fuller use of the premises. He was an excellent cook and introduced a number of young professional musicians, some of whom are now well-known, to direct courses for him. He brought a large number of new faces to Benslow and made a significant contribution in the struggle to 'Save Benslow' and to its later development.

Ruth Maguire

ROYAL COLLEGE OF MUSIC
Prince Consort Road, London, S.W.7
By kind permission of the Director

Saturday, 3rd November, 1962
at 3 p.m.

THE RURAL MUSIC SCHOOLS
ASSOCIATION
President: The Earl of Harewood

presents a concert given in honour of
Miss MARY IBBERSON, O.B.E.
Founder of the Association on the occasion of her retirement from the office of Director

MARGARET RITCHIE	GRAYSTON BURGESS
soprano	*counter-tenor*
ADRIENNE HALL	IAN PARTRIDGE
soprano	*tenor*
MAUREEN LEHANE	CHRISTOPHER KEYTE
contralto	*baritone*

CHOIR and ORCHESTRA drawn from
RURAL MUSIC SCHOOLS

Conductor
SIR ADRIAN BOULT
PROGRAMME 5/-

Saturday, 3 November 1962, Programme of concert in honour of Mary Ibberson.

Left to right, Edith Grubb, Mary Ibberson, Margaret Ritchie, November 1962.

The Gramophone Club

I used to go to the Gramophone Club. I was living at Kings Walden then and I used to go straight from work and someone would give me a lift home. It was a big club and about fifty or sixty people met there each month. People brought their own records and each month someone different led the group and gave a talk. Our equipment was very good quality and was kept at Benslow.

Kay Petrie

The Benslow Effect, 1965

The spell of the recorder and its music really gripped me during the early years of my marriage to Elaine. She, of course, was an excellent violinist, so I was rather surprised to find she also had a liking for the humble recorder. With her I went to some meetings of the Society of Recorder Players, at various country houses, and came to realise the potentialities of the instrument. With it, I discovered, one could carve sublime melodies – arcs of sound that stood up in the air, self-supporting and glowing! Moreover, with the recorder one could enter into a simple kind of chamber music formerly reserved for string players, a hallowed few who had learnt to play in childhood.

It was for such a meeting of the Society of Recorder Players that I first went to Little Benslow Hills – a strangely inappropriate name for the large house at Hitchin, where there are no hills but the Rural Music School Association had its headquarters. (Under a different name, in 1997 it still flourishes.)

Well, as I approached the front door I looked across to the right, where a smooth green lawn stretched across to a row of tall trees bounding a copse. But isolated in the grassy plain was a single tree, under which a group of people were assembled. Then came the wonderful moment; a mellifluous sound of music came drifting over the sunlit lawn to my ears. A sweet, yet dignified melody supported by a harmonic web, that weaved in and out, and floated over the green carpet to me as I stood by the door, about to enter for the first time the friendly house where I subsequently was to spend many happy hours.

That tree has gone now, and Walter Bergmann (who was conducting the players) has gone the way of all flesh. Little Benslow Hills survives, thriving. But still in my memory lives that magical moment when the sound of recorders in consort floated to my ears across the sunlit grass.

Leslie Minchin (My Footsteps Through the Century)

The Macnaghten Quartet

From 1956 we worked in Cambridge for eleven years and lived in Saffron Walden. Then our viola player had to give up and at the same time our children had left home and we no longer needed a large house. So in 1967, once again, we contacted various people, including Helen Wright, who wrote back and said, 'If you are thinking of going anywhere – come here.'

We were interviewed at Highbury House by David Wells, who was the Hertfordshire County Music Adviser and Music Director of the Hertfordshire Rural Music School – he had a dual role and the County Council paid his salary. He was very keen, he had vision and could see where it could lead. John Railton was Assistant County Music Adviser, mostly for North Herts, based at Highbury House. He then became the first Director of Music at Hitchin College of Further Education.

We were appointed as tutor/performers, with an ordinary teacher's week, during which we had to spend two fifths of the time playing and three fifths teaching. We went to different schools, including infants' schools, mostly in North Hertfordshire which was the most deprived, musically speaking because it was too far from London. We reached out to a lot of people. Part of our work was coaching strings for the Youth Orchestra. There was very little violin teaching because the people who did it would have to be resident – it was not worth coming from London.

I didn't do any teaching at all until I was fifty and came to Cambridge (Barking was education not teaching). In Hitchin I taught at Hitchin Girls' Grammar School and a Catholic primary school in Letchworth. I had never done any class teaching before, but you can't teach violin in class, it is an individual thing. I had to do six pupils in an hour, not too bad. After a bit an Irish nun, the headmistress of the primary school gave me carte blanche.

Anne Macnaghten

A Sad Year

The deaths of both Ethne Pryor and Edith Grubb made 1968 a sad year for Mary Ibberson. She visited Edith every day during the illness that preceded her death on 20 January, and then continued to live alone at Fieldfares.

Retirement of Helen Wright

This is the moment to realise and to remember with gratitude what Helen Wright has done for the Rural Music Schools Association and therefore for all Rural Music Schools in England for thirty years… Helen had had no professional training as a musician and had in fact graduated at Cambridge in modern languages and subsequently spent three years in Rome in a Foreign Office secretarial post. But she was highly sensitive to music, became an expert recorder player and believed in what the RMSA was trying to do.

There are those who believe that all musical organisations should be run by non-musicians. This is perhaps an extreme view, but it is certain that all such organisations are the better for having on their staff someone who has enough sense, administrative capacity and humour to keep musicians straight. Helen has always been a leading example of the wisdom of this policy. We shall probably never know how many tangles of other people's confused reasoning she untied, how many crooked paths she made straight, how many near-disasters she re-steered to success; but we do know that she became a wonderful second-in-command to Mary Ibberson, and for the last eight years has fulfilled with distinction the almost impossible job of succeeding her as Director…

Mervyn Bruxner (Making Music, Number 74, Autumn 1970)

Jean Salder

In 1969, Jean Salder was appointed Director of the RMSA to succeed Helen Wright. From 1956 to 1963 he had been Director of the Cornwall Rural Music School, where he and his wife, Dulcie, had achieved a considerable extension of musical activities. Since 1963 he had been Lecturer in Music at Wolverton College of Further Education, Bletchley, Buckinghamshire.

The Suzuki Method of Violin Teaching

A workshop and concert was held at the Royal College of Music, London, on Saturday, 3 October 1970, arranged by the Schools Music Association.

The ten young students, aged seven to twelve, from Dr Simichi Suzuki's Talent Educational School in Japan, with their teachers, came to London via Germany en route for Portugal and the United States – a 34-day tour in all, and the first to include Europe…

Put simply, the plan seems to be to start at the age of three, with the practical involvement of the parents – this is essential… There must be constant listening to music, even if only as 'background' music… Pupils play by ear and imitation for three or four years, notation comes later… Individual lessons are given to every child, but playing with others (in unison) is encouraged from the start… There is careful supervision of practice and ensemble by parents and teacher. Pupils are taught to work hard from the beginning… The question remains for all of us who play and teach in this country: How can we best adapt these ideas to our environment?

Gertrude Collins (Making Music,
Spring 1971)

Suzuki Method – £27,000 grant

The Suzuki method aroused considerable interest and conflicting reactions from music teachers, who concluded that further investigation was necessary. In 1971 the RMSA was delighted to announce that, in co-operation with the Hertfordshire Local Education Authority and the Hertfordshire County Music School, they would undertake a five-year study into the method, beginning in September 1972. The cost of the investigation, including training selected teachers and buying instruments, was paid from generous grants by the Leverhulme Trust Fund and the Calouste Gulbenkian Foundation. Chairman of the Steering Committee was Mary Ibberson.

Why so Interested?

What was it that caused the RMSA to be so interested in the 'method'? We had seen reports of success and failure in other countries and we had seen the film 'Happy Children of Japan' which made us determined to to oppose the introduction of the method into this country. The turning point was the Workshop and Concert sessions at the Royal College of Music... These were no regimented oriental robots, but highly individual youngsters, enjoying every minute of their playing...What is the 'Suzuki method'? If each of its points is taken separately we find that they are very much the same as those applied by any good teacher since string teaching began, the only difference being that they are applied to a greater degree...There is no doubt that in the early stages of instruction, the teachers will have to keep the pupils' age always in their mind, and exercise a tremendous amount of patience. Can this method work in this country?... We hope to give...regular progress reports of the work in future issues of Making Music.

Jean Salder (Making Music, Autumn 1971)

CHAPTER 5

New Concert Hall

Financial Problems

Industrial unrest, oil shortages, the three-day working week, inflation galloping to a record 25%, bitter conflict in Northern Ireland, the 'Winter of Discontent', the depredations of Dutch elm disease: such were the headlines of the 1970s. At the Ordinary General meeting of the RMSA Council on 7 December 1970, the Treasurer, Russell Scott, presented accounts which showed a loss of £2,608 on the General and

Little Benslow Hills accounts, against which Miss Sybil Eaton had raised £312 for the Knocker Fund. However, the financial problem was to be solved by the sale of land at Little Benslow Hills.

Between 1969 and 1971 the RMSA was engaged in prolonged legal negotiations to sell a piece of land at Benslow which backed on to a large garden in Chiltern Road, the owner of which wished to sell it for housing development. A number of proposals were discussed, including one in 1970 in which a developer put forward detailed plans to demolish the house at Little Benslow Hills and develop the whole site. It was suggested that the RMSA could either have a new, purpose-built headquarters there, or move to more suitable premises elsewhere. An undated, unsigned note, possibly by Helen Wright as it is typed on the back of a letter addressed to her, and found in a file for March 1970, appears to have been sent to Mary Ibberson about the proposal:

'I don't want this'

It's not my decision of course – but I am quite sure I don't want this. The partial development as originally thought of, yes.

If we do the Bovis thing we shall lose all the attraction this place has for its customers. I was impressed again last w/e, where we had a lot of new people, by the effect the hall fire and general welcoming atmosphere of the 'old fashioned' and the peaceful and beautiful garden has on them. The old customers came not only for technical tuition, but for the balm to the tired spirits! We should only have to offer a tidy, efficient house inferior in size to similar things available elsewhere…'

Unsigned, undated letter, to 'M.I.' possibly by Helen Wright, March 1970

Sale of Land

The large-scale development plans came to nothing and the sale of 1.6 acres backing on to Chiltern Road was agreed on 29 September 1971, for the sum of £26, 871. Preservation orders had been placed on the trees, but an ancient wych elm, considered possibly partially diseased, was felled to make way for the development.

It was against this background that the RMSA Council took the decision to build a recital room at Benslow. In all the years since the movement was founded in 1929 the RMSA had never had a concert hall of its own.

A Frustrating time

As a clarinettist (but at that time a director in industry) who was a close friend of Jean Salder, the Director of the Rural Music Schools Association, I became a Council member in 1971/2, and apart from a gap from 1977 to 1981 sat on Council until 1992. As I was in industry, I was invited on to both the Fund Raising Committee and the Building Committee to plan and construct the RMSA's first recital room. This was a frustrating time for everyone because of inflation, the Israeli-Egypt war and the decline of the pound, leading to a UK financial crisis.

Donald Clark

An Act of Faith

Mary Ibberson was very much in favour of building the recital room. At one Council meeting, when the financial difficulties of the project were made only too clear, a vote had to be taken as to whether or not to continue with it. Mary Ibberson went very quiet and then said, 'I think it has to be an act of faith.'

Cakes in the Auditorium

Council at the time included Lady Bonham Carter, Lady Chandos, Bernard Shore who was a tour-de-force in the English string world, Helen Wright who was the previous Director and Helen Brunner. Mary Ibberson sat on the Policy Committee and, of course, lived in Fieldfares. In the 1970s, Council frequently met in the Royal College of Music, as David Willcocks was Principal, while Vice-President of RMSA. Yehudi Menuhin was our president at the time. Annual General Meetings were held in the auditorium of John Lewis & Co. Ltd. in Oxford Street, with most delightful confections and cakes provided by John Lewis.

Donald Clark

Five to a Bedroom

I first went to Little Benslow Hills in 1971 for a weekend of Elementary Orchestra under Agnes Best. The price for the Friday to Sunday had just gone up from four guineas to six, and the atmosphere was friendly, informal and Spartan.

The orchestra played in what is now the dining room, which was quite a squeeze. (The new Recital Hall was just about to be built.) We seemed to get through an amazing amount of music, and Miss Best was an encouraging and very kindly conductor. I remember asking her about the origins of the Rural Music Schools and her telling us that she had been one of the original music teachers who went round the country to schools in out of the way places.

There were about five to a bedroom, and bathrooms were few and far between. We all ate at one long table in the dining room – now the sitting room next to the bar. The food was simple and not very plentiful. I remember very small helpings of macaroni cheese being doled out by a matron-like figure at the head of the table.

There was a rota for washing up, and everyone cleared their own crockery, etc. We

used to gather in the kitchen in the evening to make cocoa or coffee and chat before going to bed.

Daphne Hope

Recital Room Appeal

Lady Redcliffe-Maud was chairman of Council at this time. Her husband, Master of University College, Oxford, had recently become a household name as chairman of the commission which produced the 'Maud Report,' whose controversial recommendations for redrawing the county boundaries of England and Wales were put into effect on 1 April 1974. In the same year he came to the rescue of the Benslow recital room project. In one appeal letter, he wrote, 'We think it wrong to postpone building or wait for costs to escalate still further. So we are going ahead, in faith that when the bills come you and our other well-wishers will help to pay for them.'

The Worse Things Become, The More Music is Needed

With our country's financial situation worsening, we members of the Council were fearful, though we knew in our hearts that the worse things became the more music was needed. Our doubts were finally overcome by our Chairman's faith and enthusiasm, and when she told us that Lord Redcliffe-Maud had promised to be Chairman of the Appeals Committee, we knew that we could not fail. No-one will ever know how hard he worked for us. Coming at that inauspicious time even he had an uphill job; but though the full scheme had to be postponed we were to have our Hall. Once the decision was made things happened quickly. On learning at the Annual general Meeting last November [1974] that the Hall would be ready by May, our President, Yehudi Menuhin, got out his diary and gave us his first free date, May 27th 1975, and our Chairman promptly asked him to play the Bach Chaconne and we were away.

Sybil Eaton,
at the opening of the Peter Morrison Hall
(RMSA Annual Report, 1975)

The Peter Morrison Recital Room

On some days everything seems to go wrong; on others, metaphorically, the sun shines from dawn to dusk. Such a day was May 27th 1975, when the new Peter Morrison recital Room was

opened at Little Benslow Hills by Yehudi Menuhin, President of the Rural Music Schools Association. The most careful and imaginative preparations had been made for the success of the day and Jean and Dulcie Salder and the staff of Little Benslow Hills are to be congratulated on the smooth running of all arrangements. Special mention must be made of the exquisite flower arrangements by Lady Redcliffe-Maud. The beautiful new hall was filled to capacity by the large gathering of people associated over many years with the RMS movement...

The Recital Room, designed by Mr Simon de C. Bennett is named after Mr Peter Morrison in recognition of his generosity and encouragement which made the whole project feasible. He is well-known for his love of music; as a member of the Council of the Royal College of Music (at which in 1912 he won an open scholarship), as a member of the Council of the Royal Albert Hall,

Arcade from the house to the Peter Morrison Recital Hall, on right. (Courtesy Juliet Abrahamson)

and as a keen pianist all his life, he has combined his devotion to music with his very successful business career. For his services to music he was awarded the OBE in 1972.

Muriel Anthony,
'The Peter Morrison Recital Room'
(Making Music, Number 89, Autumn 1975)

Medau Courses

At the time I went to Hitchin on my first choral week-end in 1975 I was also involved in a unique form of music called 'Medau Rhythmic Movement', and the Peter Morrison Hall was the ideal place in which to hold Medau classes – a lovely clean smooth floor, (we worked in bare feet), light and airy, well heated in winter, and beautiful grounds where we could work out of doors – weather permitting! I took Beryl Smith, one of our senior Medau Teachers, along to see the then Director, and he agreed to let us use Benslow for a week-end course – having assured himself that we weren't some sort of cranky way-out organisation!

We ran the first Medau week-end in May 1976, and five or six more during the next six years or so. Catering was sometimes a problem, as we were occasionally offered a week-end booking when the catering staff were having a weekend off. On such occasions we found an outside caterer to come and feed us, and on one occasion we brought our own food and looked after ourselves.

Jean Laidlaw

The Beginning of the End?

Given the national economic problems of that time, the building of the Peter Morrison Recital Room was no small triumph for the RMSA, but there had been no planning application for public concerts and its use had to be restricted to performances within the framework of the course programme. This oversight was not realised at first and in the euphoria that followed the completion of the Recital Room, the RMSA's difficulties may have seemed for a time, to recede a little: but they would not go away. The RMSA had eventually to face not only continually rising costs, but also the beginning of the end of the system of music education that Mary Ibberson had founded. Victims of their own success and of the drive for improved state education, Rural Music Schools across the country were being first taken over by local education authorities and then abandoned as they proved too expensive to run. Perhaps no-one could yet quite face up to it, but the days of the RMSA, as then constituted, were numbered.

Call for help

Throughout the 1970s the RMSA Annual Report listed all the affiliated music centres; and as late as 1973 there was a review of each centre in the Annual Report. I saw the 'tail end' of the music centres coming under LEAs. I also, as a Council member, had to consider the natural call for help from some of these centres as they were cut back or closed down by LEAs in the late 1970s and 80s.

Donald Clark

Ibberson Way

Meanwhile, financial difficulties were being staved off by the sale of more land for houses. The builder who purchased the land

and built the three houses and the road named Ibberson Way, was David Moore. This was his earliest contact with the RMSA.

The Equation Before Us

A major change occurred on September 1st 1975, just three months after the Peter Morrison Hall was opened, when Jean Salder retired as Director and was succeeded by Geoffrey Brand. In the spring of 1976 the new Director wrote an article for Making Music, entitled *Whither the RMSA?* in which he reflected on his first few months in post, pointing out that 'It would be all too simple to argue that course fees should take care of expenditure, and so costing should be a simple matter of accounting. This is to miss the whole argument of the Association's philosophy, i.e. to provide musical opportunity and instruction to all who seek or desire it at a cost which is within reach of all... That's the equation which we must constantly keep before us... to get the answer to that wrong is to lead eventually to a situation in which, with only a small spelling change, we could be witnessing 'wither the RMSA.'

I Don't Know How I Did It

Then Geoffrey Brand took over and about this time the Music School started having lots of their own weekends. Housekeepers came and went. In the last two and a half years I took that on, cooking and so on for about fifty people. I don't know how I did it now. Geoffrey Brand was very nice. He and his wife Violet were marvellous. I liked them.

Eileen Maylin

Last Issue

The journal, Making Music, made its final appearance with the autumn 1976 issue.

The RMSA had, for many years, been supported in the publication of *Making Music* by the joint sponsorship of the Standing Conference for Amateur Music (SCAM) whose chairman, J.K. Owens, wrote, in the final issue, 'Unlike so much of our mail, *Making Music* has not been instantly consigned to the waste bin. It has been far too interesting. But all good things must come to an end. Grisly inflation has done its worst, but we are grateful to remember *Making Music*'s past successes and glad to know that some of the best features will appear in other ways... *Making Music* must perforce come to an end, but amateur music-makers have long proved their ability to adapt to changing circumstances and herein lies our hope for the future. Let us ensure that the good relations that already exist between our two organisations are strengthened rather than diminished in the years to come.'

It was reported in the same issue that, since writing this message, J.K. Owens had become chairman of the RMSA.

For Joy That We Are Here

1976 saw the completion of the Suzuki investigation which had begun in September 1972, and the publication of an impressive full Report, followed in 1977 by a briefer, summary document. At the same time Mary Ibberson was completing *For joy that we are here*, the story in her own words of the founding and subsequent development of the Rural Music School movement, which was published in November 1977 by the Bedford Square Press of the National Council of Social Service, price £2.75

She Liked Writing It

We were there when Miss Ibberson's book was published. We were excited, but I don't remember there being any kind of celebration about it. I don't think she liked any fuss about anything to do with herself. But she liked writing it, it made her happy. Mind you, she was always quite a cheerful sort of person.

Eileen Maylin

Listening to music. (Richard Dykes)

CHAPTER 6

'Little Benslow Hills to be Demolished'

A Policy Document

With true irony, just as the Suzuki Investigation Report, and Mary Ibberson's book, were showing the world what had been achieved by the movement which she founded, the RMSA Council issued, on 21 July 1977, a Policy Document which proposed that the property of Little Benslow Hills should be sold and the proceeds handed to a Trust to carry on the work of the Association in the field of music. For many, despite previous ominous financial signals, the news was almost unbelievable.

It Had Reached So Many People

So many people were anxious to save Benslow because it had reached out so far – it was partly the building. One evening in September 1977 the Oriel Singers looked very miserable and were asked, 'Whatever's happened?' They answered, 'Don't you know, this place has been put up for sale?'

Doris Gare

Dramatic Events

A dramatic situation arose at Murray Gordon's Christmas Party at Little Benslow Hills in 1977. John Power, Director of Education at Tottenham, member of the RMSA Council, objector to the proposal to sell, brought a set of papers to discuss with me. Apart from attending a few private courses at Little Benslow Hills, I had no inside knowledge of its affairs but had considerable administrative experience and the conviction that music mattered to the community. Sadly, before John had time to show me his papers he became acutely ill and leaving him in hospital I returned to the party saying that he had been reassured that we would take some action about closure. The result was a petition by members of the party to be presented by Murray and me to the Chairman, J.K. Owens. On 3 January, 1978, we met J.K. Owens, presented the petition and had an extended discussion about the future of the RMSA. We gained insight to its problems and made suggestions as to ways in which financial stability might be achieved and musical activities extended rather than curtailed. It was a friendly constructive meeting. I finally applied to become a member of the Association.

Ruth Maguire

Local Petition

Christmas weekends, run by Murray Gordon

were held regularly. I was there at Christmas 1977. Ruth Maguire and I were sitting talking about the situation and we said, 'What can we do about it?' – and we got up a petition from that weekend. We started it all. I worked locally. It so happened that a lot of large houses in Hitchin were being knocked down. There was an article in the local paper headed 'The walls come tumbling down'. The Blays kept a scrapbook. So did I. There was a lot of local coverage. I organised a local petition in January 1978, in atrocious weather.

Doris Gare

Membership Closed

On 23 January 1978 John Power wrote to J.K. Owens, nominating Ruth Maguire as a

member of the RMSA and for membership of Council. They also accepted Maurice and Jenifer Lynch, Doris Gare, Bernard and Nona Blay, Murray Gordon, Norwyn Fleming and Leslie Minchin as members of the RMSA. The Council also decided then to close the membership until the future of the RMSA was settled.

One of the Few in Favour of Us

Ruth formed a committee and held the first meeting at her house on March 12th 1978, with Maurice Lynch (who later became treasurer) and the Blays and Norwyn Fleming, Murray Gordon and me. Francis Oakes came in later. He was one of the few council members in favour of us.

Doris Gare

Francis Oakes

Francis Oakes was born in 1919 and came to London from Vienna in 1937.

An electronic and acoustic engineer, he was for many years with Ferguson Radio and eventually became Director of Research and Engineering for a subsidiary of the Thorn Group in Enfield and London. After he left them he was for about fourteen years a partner in a small and distinguished firm of engineering consultants. He retired in 1984. As an amateur musician, he played piano and oboe and took conducting lessons. He had conducted the Sebastian Singers in London and the Oriel Singers of Hitchin and was the first chairman of the Board of Trustees of the Tureck Bach Research Foundation, Oxford.

I Helped to Save Benslow

My links with Benslow started in 1951, when Mary Ibberson invited me to become a member of Council. I sang in the concert in the Albert Hall. In 1978 I helped Ruth Maguire to save Benslow from demolition and destruction.

Francis Oakes

A Breach of Trust

In March 1978, Hilary Whitfield, a friend at Letchworth, telephoned to ask whether I had heard that the RMSA proposed to sell Benslow – the house to be demolished and the land sold for a housing estate. My immediate response was disbelief – if there was such a proposal, it would never be allowed. But Mrs Whitfield insisted. Whoever was in charge at Benslow now had proposed to sell the property. Miss Seebohm's house was to be demolished, and the new hall. A group of people had tried to stop them, but a report that day in the local newspaper, The Comet, said they had failed.

So I said that if they could not put a stop to it, I would. I had organised successful campaigns, local, national and international, and I felt sure that such an outrageous plan could be stopped.

Like everyone else at that time I believed that Little Benslow Hills had been bequeathed to the RMSA by Miss Seebohm. She intended the property to be used for the purposes of the Association – for music. To sell it and demolish the house was a breach of trust. Already the local authority had broken the other trust in the will by building upon the land which Miss Seebohm intended to be 'an Open Space to which the residents of Hitchin may resort as a place of rest and quietude'. In my opinion breaching such trusts is wrong – and it must discourage other potential benefactors.

I had known Benslow all my life. Its peacefulness and beauty had been an important formative influence on me as a child. I would do anything I could to help to prevent its destruction.

First I telephoned John Myatt, an old friend and a musician, to find out what was going on. He was out, but Patsy Myatt told me that someone was organising a petition. She referred to 'asset-stripping' and said that Bernard Blay, violinist in the Macnaghten Quartet, was a key person in the opposition to it. I went to meet Bernard and Nona, and they told me what was going on.

Richard Wiggs

It was Always There

Little Benslow Hills was always there, in the background, but we had limited active involvement with it prior to learning of the RMSA Council plan to sell it. We were strongly opposed to the demolition of yet another local building of period character and historical significance and supported the view that retaining the property would better serve revived RMSA activity than its conversion by sale into a trust fund.

Bernard Blay

Anything to Convince Them

For most of my life I have been very busy playing and coaching quartets. My links with Benslow were renewed when the Macnaghten Quartet went to Hitchin (I had been working with Anne in Cambridge) at a very complex and financially difficult time at Little Benslow

Hills. We tried to organise as many weekend courses as we could; we would run them with as few as twelve players, to show the committee that the place was needed, anything to convince them that it shouldn't be closed down. It was a very difficult time but we did struggle on. A friend, a young violin student, came with me. She cooked large meals at home, brought them with her and we all worked together in the kitchen. We were all determined that Benslow should continue.

Phyllis Ebsworth

Prepared to Work for Nothing

We knew Norman Hearn who had worked with Mary Ibberson in Bermondsey. He had recently retired, but was full of energy and looking for a new outlet. We went to see him in Cambridge, discussed the position and put forward the possibility of him taking over and turning the place round. We had a little meeting here – Ruth, Maurice and I, with Norman, and he agreed to take on the honorary post. We were a group with a common objective, so we had people expert in their fields, who were prepared to work for nothing.

Bernard Blay

Local Objections

At this stage there were two distinct areas of activity. Whilst I was dealing with RMSA Council matters, Doris Gare undertook to encourage and stimulate the local community to lobby the Local Council and the Planning Department against giving consent for the destruction of one of the last remaining Victorian houses in the neighbourhood and for the development of its land for private housing. She contacted Councillors, instituted petitions, encouraged local people to write objections to the local authority, the RMSA and the Charity Commission and she was in touch with the local press.

Ruth Maguire

Getting Nowhere

The Blays told me that the petition to the RMSA Council had been politely ignored. The petition with 1,800 signatures to the North Hertfordshire District Council (NHDC) had had no effect. Nor could it – as the Council's planning staff explained, an application for demolition and 'development' (building houses, etc) could not be refused except on 'planning grounds', which means such things as inadequate access, drainage, etc.

Clearly opposition to the sale of Benslow were getting nowhere. My view was that several things must be done. I must see a copy of the Articles and Memorandum of the RMSA. Effort that was being put into such things as petitioning the NHDC should now be put into writing to the Charity Commission, urging it not to give permission for the sale. And – using the tactic I had used successfully for several campaigns – we should get all the press publicity we could.

The Blays told me that one long-time member of the RMSA Council, John Power of Ipswich, was trying to stop the sale; as was someone who had recently been accepted on to the Council, Ruth Maguire. We agreed that I would contact them.

Richard Wiggs

Planning to save Benslow

Richard Wiggs telephoned John Power, who was unwell, but was immensely pleased to hear from him and offered to send him a quantity of papers, including Council papers. Ruth Maguire told him of her efforts to persuade the Chairman, J.K. Owens, not to proceed with the sale, the stated reason for which was a relatively small annual operating deficit. She believed that, with some reorganisation of the Association's affairs, this deficit could be got rid of and she had persuaded the Council to allow her to present a five-year plan to them. Richard Wiggs suggested to her the same list of actions to be taken, that he had discussed with the Blays, but she felt it right to wait until the Chairman and Council had considered her proposals.

'Outlook Bleak'

Throughout the summer, reports appeared in the local papers with such headlines as 'Benslow Hills – Outlook Bleak', 'Music School HQ is Doomed', 'Benslow Hills Battle Lost'. Ruth told me that the RMSA Council had rejected her proposals. In the autumn, belatedly, I and some friends including Leonard Hughes and John Railton, as well as Bernard Blay and a Hitchin GP, Dr Gerald Tidy, began to write to the local papers. One of my letters became an article headlined Benslow Hills Decision 'Deplorable'.

In October I wrote to the RMSA's president, Yehudi Menuhin (who did not reply) and to the Charity Commission (which did).

Richard Wiggs

The 'Save Benslow' Committee

Late in October, John Power suggested to Richard Wiggs that, as efforts to persuade the RMSA Council to change its mind had got nowhere, a vigorous 'Save Benslow Committee' committee was needed. He also advised obtaining a copy of Esther Seebohm's will, as he had an idea that the sale of the property might not be legal.

The 'Save Benslow' Committee was set up at Richard Wiggs' house in Bedfordshire, with Ruth Maguire as chairman and Richard Wiggs as secretary. The meeting discussed what might be done at the Annual General Meeting of the RMSA in London on 6 December. Most of those present had been at an Extraordinary General Meeting

in October, and they described the difficulty of getting anything said, or done, at the meeting.

I was Prepared to go to the High Court

In the ensuing weeks I was in very close contact with J.K. Owens and with the Charity Commission. I kept J.K. Owens informed of the thinking of the Save Benslow Committee and of other supporters, whilst he shared confidential information with me. Increasingly it became clear that the impasse could only be overcome by resort to the High Court. I made it clear that I too was prepared to appear in the High Court. It was not always easy to restrain certain objectors to the 'sale' from engaging in unhelpful publicity, particularly with the press.

Ruth Maguire

We Would See

Ruth had obtained for me a copy of the RMSA's Articles and Memorandum. I found that the RMSA was a limited company, and there are rules for the conduct of company meetings. Also, non-members could attend an AGM as proxies for members. I said that I would get myself appointed as a proxy, and would go to the meeting. I was told that I would get nowhere – but I had much experience of discussions, arguments and flaming rows, on radio and television, here and in the USA. I would go to the meeting and we would see.

Various members of the RMSA who could not attend the meeting wanted to vote against the sale by proxy. I produced the proxy forms. I printed three versions. Most of them appointed, as proxy, Ruth. But in a few I inserted, instead of her name, my name; and in a few more, the name of my friend Harold Bland. I guessed that when the forms arrived at the RMSA office, with most of the 'Ruth Maguire' version on top, no-one was likely to read every one of the seemingly identical forms, and when Harold and I arrived at the meeting this would be a surprise to Council.

Also, I sent a report on the formation of the 'Save Benslow' Committee to the local papers. This produced the largest front-page headlines so far: 'New Group to Fight for Benslow'. The report urged people to write to the Charity Commission and gave the address.

Richard Wiggs

The Will

Ruth Maguire obtained the Will and sent it to Richard Wiggs. He and Leonard Hughes read it together, with increasing satisfaction. It stated that Little Benslow Hills was to be held in trust by the RMSA, 'to be used for the advancement of musical education...' but that if ever the RMSA became unable to administer this trust, it must hand over the property to other trustees who were willing to use the property for the same purpose of musical education. Richard Wiggs immediately sent a copy of the Will to the Charity Commission.

A Fateful Letter

On 5 December – the day before the AGM – someone at the Commission telephoned to dictate to me a letter which he was about to send by post, explaining the meaning of the Will. He wanted to be sure that I had the text before the AGM. The letter stated that 'It has only recently come to our attention that Little Benslow Hills is not, as we supposed, property held for the general purposes of the RMSA, but it is held upon the trusts of the will of the late Esther Margaret Seebohm. These trusts... create a separate charity and require the property to be used exclusively for the advancement of musical education in rural areas. Any decision to wind up the RMSA would not... affect the position of Little Benslow Hills, and if the Association... cannot continue to administer the property, [it] must seek other trustees willing and able to carry out the Trust contained in the Will.'

Leonard and I had been right. I typed and copied my transcript of the text as dictated, to take to the AGM. But on the 6th, the day of the meeting, the posted copy arrived, and I made copies of this.

Richard Wiggs

Uproarious AGM

The Annual General Meeting was in the board-room at John Lewis's in Oxford Street. The 'Save Benslow' group met outside. I had told some of them, by telephone, about the Charity Commission's letter, which they now all read. We were not sure whether, under company rules, I was entitled to speak in the meeting, so we agreed that at the start of the meeting, Maurice Lynch would ask the chairman's permission to read the letter.

When we approached the board-room, Harold Bland and I were noticed, and we were told we could not enter. We pointed out that we were proxies for absent members. This was received with disbelief, but eventually the proxy forms were found, we went in and the meeting began. Mr Lynch informed the chairman that he had an important letter from the Charity Commission, dated the previous day, addressed to Mr Wiggs, which indicated that the Charity Commission was not giving permission for the sale of Little Benslow Hills and asked permission to read the letter.

The chairman refused permission. He refused a motion, proposed by Leslie Minchin and seconded by Mr Lynch, that I be allowed to speak, and a further motion that the chairman leave the chair. He denied that the Charity Commission had made any statement such as that in the letter to me. I challenged this, accompanied by repeated instructions that I was not allowed to speak, and to sit down. Eventually, after twenty minutes of

argument and interruptions, and efforts by Mr Lynch, Mr Minchin and Miss Maguire to have the letter read, Mr Lynch succeeded in reading it. He even pointed out that the earlier sales of parts of Benslow's land were apparently ultra vires.

Richard Wiggs

A Microphone in an Umbrella

After the meeting, Harold Bland and I disclosed to Ruth Maguire that the main purpose of Harold coming to the meeting was to attend to a tape-recorder which we had in a shopping bag, with a microphone in a rolled-up umbrella. We had recorded the meeting, and so had evidence which could be sent to the Charity Commission, and the

Department of Trade, which regulated
company meetings.

Richard Wiggs

They Thought They Had Won

After the campaigners had received the
Charity Commission's letter they thought
they had won. There were headlines in
the local press:

CLAUSE IN WILL MAY SAVE
BENSLOW HILLS (*Comet*, 23 November
1978) But the majority on the Council
were not disposed to concede defeat. And
some members of the 'Save Benslow'

committee still hoped and believed that
they could be persuaded to drop the plan
to sell, and keep Benslow in operation.

We Had Waited Long Enough

The only sensible way to proceed was for the
Chairman and those who still supported him
to resign, and for them to be replaced by
people who really wanted to run Benslow.
But because of the split in the 'Save Benslow'
committee, the Council was allowed time to
get over the shock of the Charity
Commission's letter to me, and to start
searching for ways of getting round, or
overturning, the Seebohm will. There were
even rumours that they were planning action
in the High Court. I knew that while they
might finance such action with the RMSA's
reserve cash, to oppose them would be
prohibitively costly for us. And it would be
such a waste of time and money, if things
were allowed to get to that stage.

By the summer of 1979 John Power and I
and our supporters thought we had waited more
than long enough. We were becoming alarmed
by the scheming within the Council, so we
decided to take action. Some fierce letters from
us, including one from John Railton (drafted by
me), made the Council realise at last that if they
did embark upon legal action to circumvent
Miss Seebohm's will, numerous complaints
about the conduct of the affairs of the charity
would come out.

Richard Wiggs

She Loved the House

Miss Ibberson knew about the plan to sell
Benslow and she was worried to death, she

didn't care for it at all. It was quite a shock to her. She loved the house and she loved her bungalow.

Eileen Maylin

She Had to Accept it

We wrote to Mary Ibberson and kept in contact with her. She replied that despite everything she had to accept that Little Benslow Hills had fulfilled its function.

Bernard Blay

Letter from Mary Ibberson

A few days before the arrival of the Charity Commission's letter, Richard Wiggs had written to Mary Ibberson, to tell her about the efforts to save Benslow, and asking for her support. She replied:

Harbour House, West Bay,
Bridport, Dorset, DT6 4EY
December 3rd 1978

Dear Mr Wiggs,

Thank you for your letter and enclosures, bringing me up-to-date with the campaign you are waging with so much energy and devotion.

But I am sorry to say I think it mistaken, and cannot agree with it. I find the plan unpractical, full of wishful thinking, and as far as the detailed realities of the situation are concerned, irresponsible. Where is the skilled staff, book-keeper, typist, housekeeper, etc coming from? Where is the money to pay for much-needed repairs and maintenance of the overcrowded old house? (What would happen if there were a fire?)

The Maylins too are indispensable, but they are getting tired and older, and you cannot count on them for the future.

The financial difficulties have not been exaggerated. Deficits on running expenses have been mounting for some years. With inflation they have recently increased beyond what could be honestly accepted.

Nor do I agree that the recent leadership lacks idealism. Far otherwise. They have simply made us face the facts. They are the people who care, and who really know from experience.

However, I cannot now argue the case in detail, I can only say that I have been kept informed of all the facts and arguments since the crisis developed. I have complete confidence in the members of our Working Committee and I fully support their policy.

Needless to say, I grieve over the whole sorry business, and appreciate the feelings that inspire your Committee, though I believe them to be mistaken.
Yours sincerely and regretfully,

Mary Ibberson

Death of Mary Ibberson, 6 May 1979

The Advices admonish us to 'Face with courage the approach of old age... realising that it may bring wisdom, serenity and detachment.' These qualities were hers when, in her 80s, she retired to Harbour House on the coast of Dorset. Even here, she gathered together some of the residents to form a choir at Christmas time. Her friends – and she had many – who were able to visit her there realised that, though the 'tempo'

Little Benslow Hills is saved. Left to right: Richard Wiggs, Ruth Maguire and Maurice Lynch, July 1979.

had lessened, she was still able to give and to share from her deep spiritual resources.

From an obituary in The Friend, 1 June 1979, by Margaret Beaton

A Sad Ending

On 2 July 1979 friends and admirers of Mary Ibberson meet at St Sepulchre's church, Holborn, for an inspiring musical memorial service celebrating her life and work.

Council members then moved to their meeting held at the YMCA, Great Russell Street at 2.30 pm that same day, to receive resignations from the Vice-President, Chairman, Chairman of Finance Committee, Treasurer, other members of Council and the Director. Those remaining were John Power, Francis Oakes and me. I was appointed

chairman, Maurice Lynch to Council and to Hon. Treasurer. The Director handed me the RMSA's cheque book and the meeting was closed. A sad end on such a day.

Ruth Maguire

Why Was I So Involved?

Firstly because Mary Ibberson was a good friend of my wife. Mary said there were many elderly people on the committee and I was a young executive in industry and I knew I could help. I was involved in music all my life, it was a fundamental interest. I went to some courses for fun and enjoyed them. I liked the atmosphere and made many friends. Also, after I moved to Welwyn thirty years ago, I was closer.

Francis Oakes

Headlines

We were mentioned thirty two times in the local paper, with stories such as Norman Hearn saying, 'I'll run the Rural Music School for nothing.' We eventually saved Benslow in July 1979. Council met to dissolve itself. The headline was SAVED – BENSLOW HILLS PRESSURE GROUP WINS THE DAY.

Doris Gare

Long Term Commitment

Many people were involved in preventing the sale of Little Benslow Hills. Special mention must be made of John Power, Francis Oakes,

Richard Wiggs.

Ruth Maguire.

Maurice Lynch, Doris Gare and the Save Benslow Committee and others too numerous to mention by name who gave of their knowledge, skills and encouragement. When I embarked on the struggle I was fully aware of the responsibility involved and the long term commitment required. Mary Ibberson had been the inspiration but successive councils had given dedicated service over the years. When severe difficulties arose the membership had failed to take their responsibilities as members which – in my view – is more than just voting at meetings.

Ruth Maguire

CHAPTER 7

House Party Atmosphere

The garden in snow, early 1980s. (Courtesy Juliet Abrahamson)

A Daunting Prospect

On July 3, Maurice Lynch and I went to Little Benslow Hills to meet the staff. Mr and Mrs Maylin accepted the situation and offered to co-operate with us: they would continue their existing duties, mainly caretaking, gardening and catering for private courses that were already booked. Clerical help was available for a few hours a week and there were two part-time cleaners, one of whom, Myra, has now served the RMSA for nearly thirty years.

The buildings looked sadly neglected, the office partly cleared, boxed up ready for sale. Basic equipment throughout was poor indeed and inadequate to meet the reasonable needs of even small courses. Following a visit from the Health Inspector earlier in the year, relating to the kitchen area, the report stated *that no further courses should be arranged unless improvements were made... It was a daunting prospect.*

Ruth Maguire

Revised Membership

On 9 August 1979, Norman Hearn moved into Fieldfares, as Honorary Director of the Rural Music Schools Association, with the intention of staying for five years.

He, and the new Council, led by Ruth Maguire as Chairman, Maurice Lynch as Treasurer and with the support of an increasing number of volunteer helpers, moved rapidly into action to restore Little Benslow Hills to vibrant life. The challenge was threefold; to repair and upgrade the building; to re-instate and develop the course programme; to raise money for immediate needs and to place the RMSA on a sound financial footing for the future. To achieve these aims it would be essential to revise the RMSA's Council and membership and to give members a more direct role in fund raising. On Wednesday 5 December 1979, at an Extraordinary General Meeting of the RMSA in the auditorium of John Lewis & Co., Oxford Street, London, the following special resolution was passed:

a) The number of members of the Association to be declared unlimited.

b) Members admitted to membership after 6 December 1979 shall be liable to pay such membership subscription and shall enjoy such rights and duties as the Council may at any time and from time to time determine.

A few days later, on Sunday 11 December, at a meeting at Little Benslow Hills, the 'Save Benslow Committee' was officially wound up.

Is There Anything I Can Do?

People were extraordinarily generous once the thing started moving, with money raising and concerts. Even in the first few days people would come up to the house and say, 'Is there anything I can do?' Painting, decorating, fund-raising, persuading. The first thing I did was to clear out the entrance hall and put flowers there to make it look lived in. It was exciting, interesting to see it beginning to flower.

Ruth Maguire

It's Going to be All Right

While I was Director of Music at Oundle I took Making Music and had met Edwina Palmer and Agnes Best who lived near Ardingly College, where I was in charge. They did some teaching for me there. I knew about the Rural Music Schools Association, but had not been to Benslow.

We sent our daughter to the Friends' School at Saffron Walden. I am an admirer of the Quakers having first met them when rescuing someone from the Nazis in Vienna in 1938. One Parents' Day I again met Norman Hearn, whose daughter was also there. He was then Director of Music at the Cambridgeshire College of Arts and Technology. When Norman retired and took over at Benslow as volunteer director, I opted to come on one of his string weekends, with some hesitation. As I came in the door and saw Norman pushing a trolley with bottles of drink I thought, 'Ah! It's going to be all right.' Norman said, 'Look, I'm trying to get this place going again, would you like to join the council?' I said, 'Yes.'

Robin Miller

Fundraising Activities

The problem of permission for public concerts in the Peter Morrison Recital Room was overcome when the Hitchin Urban District Council granted a license with the proviso that additional car-parking space must be made available within one year. The Urban District Council had

'Spring' in St Francis window, Director's office. (Courtesy Juliet Abrahamson)

supported the 'Save Benslow Campaign' although it had no power to take direct action, and some councillors were now anxious to be as helpful as possible. The ability to hold fund-raising events at Benslow was a great benefit, and augmented the concerts that supporters were holding in London and elsewhere. Seizing the opportunity offered by the extensive press coverage given to the 'Save Benslow Campaign' Nona Blay set up the Benslow Music Club for local people.

The Oriel Singers

The newly formed Benslow Music Club gives its second concert in the Peter Morrison Room at Little Benslow Hills [on Sunday 9th December, 1979], with the Oriel Singers as the artistes ... The Oriel singers, with just a dozen or so members, have been in existence since the 1950s, specialising in madrigals, but also keeping their hands in with other music... Carols old and modern feature in their forthcoming concert and you will have plenty of opportunity to join in. Accompanist Rosalind Willson and conductor Margaret Johnson will also play a piano duet during the evening.

Benslow Music Club press release

Benslow Music Club

I started the club with the encouragement of Norman Hearn... The object was to bring in the local musical public by using the Peter Morrison Recital Room for public concerts (and not just for the benefit of the courses) and to give a platform to local musicians, all of whom were prepared to give their services in a great fundraising effort.

The concerts took place on Sunday evenings and lasted for about an hour. They were followed by a gathering in the house with drinks and biscuits laid on by Janet Flavell, a local singer and teacher. In the second year we introduced craft exhibitions, which contributed to what had become a popular social event. The club was discontinued in 1983.

Nona Blay

Plastering is difficult

In September 1979 there was an appeal for help to get the house ready to re-open. I told Norman Hearn I could help, but only with a seven-year-old in tow. He got her to re-plaster the the lower areas of the very top landing. He didn't say that plastering was difficult! I don't remember whether I achieved much. It was the first time I met his daughter, now Juliet Abrahamson, also on Council. Another daughter, Phyllida, fed us – and well.

Anne Conchie

A Champagne Supper

On January 12th 1980 our first public fund raising concert, a Champagne Supper was held, Christopher Bunting and Peter Croser giving their services. In June of that year a concert in the grounds of St Paul's Walden was organised by David Moore. In October with the great help of Sybil Eaton the Parikian Piano Trio gave a concert at the invitation of the Luton Music Club in the Luton Library Complex which raised a goodly sum and much local interest in our work. It was through our links with the Radcliffe Trust that ultimately gave the money

'Winter' in St Francis window, Director's office. (Courtesy Juliet Abrahamson)

to set up courses for String Teachers that Murray Gordon and I met Manoug Parikian and it was through him that we engaged the Alberni Quartet to run the first Radcliffe Trust Course. This quartet have been generous and loyal to us to this day. Encouragement was given to various groups to hire our facilities and out of these local links the Benslow Association emerged that over the years has raised a great deal of money, gifts and volunteer workers and an all-important source of publicity.

Ruth Maguire

House-party Atmosphere

As courses were re-instated, students began to return, and were charmed by the

Left to right: Anne Macnaghten, Elizabeth Lebrecht and -?-, 1998. (Howard Davis)

'informal, house party atmosphere.' Many have said that they felt entirely at home, enjoyed helping out in the kitchen and accepted with good humour the limitations of shared bedrooms which doubled as practice rooms. In an age when smokeless zones and central heating were rapidly becoming the norm, the open wood fires at Benslow provided a thrill of pleasurable nostalgia, which seemed entirely to compensate for any shortcomings in the domestic arrangements. The garden and grounds were a delight. Although not as extensive as they had been when William Ransom built the house, they still contained many of his beautiful trees and plants, providing sanctuary for wildlife and a haven of tranquillity for humans.

Enjoyment is the key

The idea in the beginning was for everyone to have a go – 'For joy that we are here.' Listening is part of that and committed local members of the Benslow Association are still ensuring a series of afternoon concerts, social occasions as much as musical, where enjoyment is the key.

Sarah Graham

Change and conflict

The idyll could not last. The amazing, almost superhuman, effort expended by those who had saved Benslow from destruction and then turned it into a thriving centre for music education, began to take its toll, as the extent of the work still to be done was realised. Although so much had been achieved, it was now necessary to look to and plan for the future and, inevitably, there were different views of the way forward. Some members of Council saw that the informal, unstructured approach to life could not continue: others saw it as the central feature of Benslow's attraction.

There were personality clashes and tensions, yet all concerned were striving for the same ends; the success of the movement which Mary Ibberson had founded and the conservation of its home, Little Benslow Hills. One thing was clear, that there was too much work for one Director to do, even with the generous and unstinting help and support of his family. A young Assistant Director, Michael Procter, was appointed to help on a part-time basis.

A Marvellous performance

The large audience at Benslow Music Club on Sunday night was treated to a marvellous performance of Dvorak's A major Piano Quintet by Nona Blay and the North Herts String Quartet. It was indeed as fine a performance as one could wish to hear in which interpretive and technical elements were ideally combined. Nona Blay is a pianist well able to match the musical and technical complexities of the work and one could only but admire the brilliance with which she performed the final Allegro. She had excellent support from her colleagues.

John Humphries, review in local paper

I Fell in Love with the Place

In 1981, I was asked to help by an elderly trustee living in Benslow Lane. Subsequently, I became chairman of the newly formed small executive committee, which took over the day-to-day running of the place from the large Council. Huge changes took place during this period, for instance, we ran appeals. I was able to do this because of my mixture of business and council experience – but I fell in love with the place. My sons allowed me to take early retirement, I had spare time and I rediscovered my music.

David Moore

A Willing band

When we started up we had a lot of voluntary help. Our secretary, Jennifer Wesley, was extremely good and worked hard. Also five people came in regularly to help, in the office. We also had to write to all former members. We got out the cards of people who had been to courses before, to send them details. We had a band of helpers, up to ten at a time to write addresses on envelopes. One day when a course was coming two of us scrubbed out the kitchen. We made marmalade. There were lots of apples and mulberries in the garden: we froze those. I was on the Council then. At one stage I was on the executive committee and I was the only woman after Ruth had resigned the chairmanship. In 1983 I resigned from all committee work anywhere.

Doris Gare

The Amateurs' Exchange

I was on the council for about five years. One thing I started was the Amateurs' Exchange (for example an orchestra in need of, say, a double bass player for a particular concert

83

Anne Conchie (Council member) checking course details, in the office, formerly the Director's office. (Courtesy Simon Baker).

might find one through the Amateurs' Exchange list). We sent circulars off to everyone we could think of, then heard about the American version, Amateur Chamber Music Players Inc., which is much bigger and worldwide. We published a booklet every so often to update it but it is now on computer.

Robin Miller

We Ran it Like a Family

My father, Norman Hearn, ran Boys' Clubs in Bermondsey during the war. He started the

Music Department of Cambridgeshire College of Arts and Technology and ran it for twenty seven years. He also did some conducting and played the organ.

I graduated from the Royal College of Music and taught singing and piano. In 1980 I was living in the USA and wanting to come back to England. I rang my father and asked if he had any contacts. He said, 'You can come and work for me, if you like'. He had been working at Benslow in an honorary capacity for at least a year by then and he was really asking me to come and help him run it, to take over the domestic arrangements of the house. He had just lost the Maylins who had retired and the Lodge was left empty. He couldn't do the whole thing himself, and so we came, in July 1980. My husband Robert-Louis was doing his PhD thesis in English and we had one child aged two. We moved into the Lodge, which was fairly sparsely furnished: we had my sister's grand piano, a bed and a couple of items of furniture until our stuff came from the USA later. It was new and exciting.

I was immediately plunged into catering for fifty people, learning on the job. I read up catering, asked other people and learnt the hard way how to economise. We had some very good paid, part-time cooks who were a great help. We became well known for catering for people's individual needs.

There was a course almost every weekend. Whereas now two or three small courses may be run at the same time, for economy, in those days if numbers were low the course still went ahead. The Macnaghten Quartet courses were always full. We had a mixture of people. It was incredibly happy, we had very little difficulty, we ran it like a family – we were a family after all.

My father was very well liked, easy going, welcoming, made people feel good. He was a handyman too, making cupboards, slapping a coat of paint on… it was not always very beautiful but a there was a huge amount to do. So I did all the furnishings. I used to go down to the market and bully the market people to let me have, for example, a Victorian chest of drawers for very little. Robert-Louis took on one of most arduous jobs, locking up at night, so there was someone in residence. It was £30 per week, not much for a family to live on but we did live in the house for free.

Juliet Abrahamson

Mulberry wine

On the second weekend in September 1980, I came to Benslow for a weekend of string playing, conducted by Norman Hearn. Without thinking, I parked my car under the mulberry tree on the Friday evening. On the next afternoon I had a look at it and found that the tree was dripping with extremely ripe mulberries – all over the car.

As a keen winemaker I thought that I just couldn't let these go to waste. So I went and found Robert Abrahamson and together we filled a sack with about ten pounds of them, with them dripping all over us as we did so. Out of this ten pounds of mulberries I made what turned out to be five gallons of extremely good wine. About eighteen months later I came to Benslow for the Annual General Meeting. It had struck me that the wine really belonged to Benslow, so I took a dozen or so bottles with me. For 50p, participants could buy a 'sample' glass with their lunch and a chance in a raffle for the remaining bottles. This all went as planned and there were three bottles left at the end, which we auctioned. For them we got £6 per bottle, quite a high price for wine in those days.

Robin Miller

I Loved the Garden

I loved the garden and walked round it every morning. Once we were having a concert in the Peter Morrison Room on a glorious summer evening, and a little muntjac deer came and stood at the end of the lawn, looking at the people and the people all looking out at him. When we told the pianist afterwards, he said, 'There was a point in the evening when I felt that no one was listening to me.'

Some time after we came here Peter Morrison's gold Rolls Royce rolled up to the door. He brought two sets of trains and gave them to the children and said, 'Who loves Uncle

Lounge and St Francis (Directors's office) from the garden, early 1980s. (Courtesy Juliet Abrahamson)

The Lodge in snow, early 1980s. (Courtesy Juliet Abrahamson)

Peter?' They were so excited. He was glad his hall was saved – it was nearly pulled down five years after it was built.

Robert-Louis also dealt with the bar and that sort of thing. I tried to make the house look good as well. When we came it was very institutionalised with four, five or six people in a fairly spartan room and few washing facilities. But everybody helped, a bit like a youth hostel or a guide camp. People were not served as in a hotel. My son, Neil, was running around, talking to everyone.

All the rooms seemed to have a general colour scheme of maroon and grey, very drab. No money had been spent on the place for a long time, not that I had any money to spend, but I did try to do something. For instance, when I first went into the dining room it had strip lighting, which is not very nice, certainly not

nice to play music by. I went to London and found five globe lights with brass fittings. Later, looking at old photographs in the cellar, I found one of the dining room with five globe lights and brass fittings!

Juliet Abrahamson

86

CHAPTER 8

Benslow Music Trust

Left to right; Norman Hearn, Lady Barbirolli, Michael Procter at the 60th Anniversary celebrations, July 1989.

Agreeing to Differ

The thrifty, self-help ethos of the immediate post-crisis era was followed by a sometimes difficult transformation to a more affluent and, to some, apparently more profligate period. There was a long transition from what has been described as 'the simple feudal system' which operated in Mary Ibberson's life-time, through a reformed management structure to the current complexity of council, committees and specialist groups. This was not achieved without strife. Change was often preceded by anguish and accomplished with tears. Council meetings occasionally seemed to consist of individuals playing different tunes, passionately and with deep feeling. Consensus was sometimes difficult to achieve, yet Francis Oakes could say, with quiet satisfaction, 'What is important is that we have had these disagreements but they have not destroyed us. We have come through them. All organisations have them. Success is not about agreeing but about agreeing to differ.'

A Walnut Tree in Memory

I left working here in 1986, did some teaching and also went on Council and have been on it ever since, apart from a couple of short periods, when I returned to help out. My father, Norman Hearn, always intended to stay for five years only. He did a lot of digging and vegetable growing and was very fit, but he died later of cancer. A walnut tree was planted in his memory.

There used to be, in my father's time, a sense that the community was running Benslow – you could walk into the dining room and there would be several local people stuffing envelopes, or the same in the library, *others mowing the lawn or helping in the kitchen. That gradually disappeared as the place was pulled into the twentieth century, and although it was right and proper that it should be, there was always a sight feeling of regret for those comfortable and informal times.*

Juliet Abrahamson

Raising the Profile

With Michael Procter as full-time director from 1983, courses began to reflect some of his own enthusiasms, particularly for choral and early music. The Baroque Opera project was one of his creations which has enjoyed continuing success, with annual Baroque courses and, in recent years, performances at The Queen Mother Theatre in Hitchin.

Baroque Opera Project, 1992, rehearsal for 'Cupid and Death.'

Jazz Week, February 1989, left to right; Chris Barnes, Jim Hawthorne, Bill Bates.

Michael Procter's vision for the new Benslow was to raise its profile in the music world. Another of his innovations was the formation of Euro-Musica, a partnership between the Benslow Music Trust and music organisations in France, Germany, Holland and Belgium. The intention was to liaise over festivals and events that were outside normal course programmes and to give amateur musicians the opportunity to take part in international music.

The newly-formed 'Benslow Music Trust' acquired official recognition on 18 July 1986, when a Certificate of Incorporation was signed under the Companies' Act, confirming that 'Rural Music Schools Association having by special resolution changed its name, is now incorporated under the name of Benslow Music Trust', with a council consisting of the Honorary Treasurer and not fewer than fifteen and not more than thirty other members of the Association.

Change of name

During this period the the RMSA had been preparing itself for a future in which adult residential music courses would become virtually its sole aim and purpose.

Artist-in-Residence

In the early 1980s my mother needed the support of nursing care and came to the Benslow Nursing Home. The Benslow coincidence was benign. I had recently started work with musicians and approached Michael Procter with the idea of developing some sort of informal artist-in-residence project at Benslow. He liked the idea and it took off. There was no question of a salary, it was simply an opportunity. I had no permanent room, but was able to stay on any course, coming into any practice room or rehearsal. Michael would have warned people at the start of a course with, 'Don't bother about Sarah,' and it was an invaluable chance for me to learn to work unobtrusively. I hope I did!

Many drawings were given to performers, coaches, visitors and there were always some on sale to course members, Benslow and myself sharing the proceeds. Two sets of cards resulted. It was a very rich time for me. I was in a special position, neither a member of staff nor a member of a course. The domestic staff knew me well and I felt I really belonged and fifteen years later I still feel really strongly attached.

Sarah Graham

Inspired by Benslow

A number of artists have been inspired by Benslow, including Carole Aston, whose evocative pictures of the house and grounds have raised many hundreds of pounds for the Music Trust. Her husband, Tony, first as Chairman of the Finance Committee and subsequently as Hon. Treasurer, has contributed significantly to the financial management of the organisation.

The Pamela Maud Wing

In the early 1980s, plans were made to provide much-needed additional residential accommodation at Benslow, by altering and extending the old coach house or even, some hoped, by building a completely new wing. As ever, raising the money was not easy and when, in 1984, discussion began over the possibility of transferring the Editha Knocker Violin Loan Scheme to Benslow, there were those who thought that it might solve the financial problem. This was not so although the Loan Scheme did come under the administrative control of Benslow, but as a separate charity. The plan to extend the old coach house was carried out, with generous help from Lord and Lady Redcliffe Maud, and the building named after their daughter, Pamela, who had died young.

Afternoon Concerts

The Music Club for local people, which Nona Blay had run successfully between 1979 and 1983, was revived in spirit in 1988, when Nona introduced a series of afternoon concerts, under the aegis of the Benslow Association. From the income they produced, the Association was able to provide money for curtains, chairs, a new piano and other items in the Peter Morrison Hall. Eric Williams, one of the most loyal and committed Benslow volunteers, gave invaluable help by distributing posters and carrying out other essential, practical work. His death in 1999 was a great blow, still keenly felt by his many friends at Benslow.

Superb Professional Concerts

Professional musicians regularly and generously give fundraising concerts at

Benslow, bringing superb music to the people of Hitchin and north Hertfordshire. Those who help in this way include the Alberni, Maggini, Medici, Coull and Sorrel Quartets and individuals such as David Campbell, Margaret Archibald, Christopher Hyde White and Jane Dodd. Many of the performers also act as course tutors, giving encouragement and inspiration to the amateur players who learn from them.

Three Hands at the Piano, Sunday 16 October, 1994

Performing will be local musician and teacher Kate Elmitt and John Railton.

John who studied at the Royal Academy of Music, was Director of Music at North Herts College. After losing his left arm following treatment for a tumour, he studied the repertoire of music composed for one hand,

Back row, left to right: Brian Muskett, Selene Mills, David Moore, Helen Marshall. Front row: Sylvia Norman, Sandra Wilkins, Michael Procter, in the early 1990s.

Valerie Hawkes, student at an Orchestral Summer School, run by Keith Stent.

including the Ravel concerto and Britten *Diversions* which he adapted for the right hand. Kate also studied at the Royal Academy and by the age of twelve had given her first radio concert broadcast at the Festival Hall. By fourteen she had attained her Performer's LRAM and with the aid of numerous prizes and awards she studied in Arezzo and Vienna. The combined skills of Kate and John have delighted audiences in the Queen Elizabeth Hall, on BBC Radio and Television and in the Far East and Australia.

Press cutting, local newspaper

100th Concert

Monday 10 June 1996 – Afternoon Concert 3.30 – Peter Maundrell (piano) Schubert, Chopin, Gershwin... Today we celebrated my 100th concert for Benslow! So glad it was Peter Maundrell who was playing.

Nona Blay

Extending the Range of Courses

In 1989, Helen Marshall joined the staff as Assistant to the Director and Secretary of the Benslow Musical Instrument Loan Scheme. Some six months later Michael Procter became ill, with a tumour in his left arm. In the difficult period of his absence Helen and Selene Mills, the Registrar coped with the work. After treatment, Michael Procter recovered and was able to return to Benslow for two years.

His successor, Keith Stent, took on a newly-styled appointment, Part-time

Orchestral Summer School, 1990s. (Courtesy Keith Stent)

Harp summer school, 1995/6. (Courtesy Keith Stent)

An Introduction to Tudor Music course. Extreme right, front, Francis Roads, tutor, 1996. (Courtesy Keith Stent)

Music Adviser. He had recently retired as chief examiner for the worldwide examinations system of Trinity College of Music, but had also served for nine years as adviser for the extensive adult education music service of the Inner London Education Authority and had much experience as tutor and conductor of amateur music societies. His Benslow duties were alongside such work and he continued as a conductor at Trinity College together with freelance duties for the Yamaha organisation and music publisher.

As a music educator, he was anxious to enlarge the range of courses and added activities which reflected the interests of the closing years of the century, such as Big Band, light orchestra, electronic keyboard, jazz guitar and music technology.

He also developed accredited courses specifically for senior piano teachers from the Far East, who were prepared to travel to this country to be taught by Associated Board teachers. Overseas students were also attracted to the Benslow International Summer Schools.

When Keith Stent left in March 1998, to head the music department at a music publisher's, Helen Marshall, who had worked very closely with both Michael Procter and Keith Stent, put forward a staff restructuring proposal, which was accepted.

Expectations are Higher

My priority has always been to respond to the needs of the customer. In 1999, I was able to draw on responses to a Membership Questionnaire which asked for members'

International Course, April 1997. Standing, extreme right, Timothy Barratt one of the course tutors.

Community Band Week, 1997.

opinions on many aspects of the music programme. The results demonstrated that people's expectations are now far higher and Benslow must keep abreast if it is going to survive in the market place.

Helen Marshall

Special Atmosphere

Benslow has played a big part in my musical life, and I have attended many courses there since 1975, mostly choral, but also Medau, Alexander, and T'ai chi. It is a lovely place, with a very special atmosphere, and it was a great relief when the threat of closure was lifted. It would have been a tragedy, and a great loss to amateur, and professional, music making.

Jean Laidlaw

New Kitchen

Improvements to the house were made in 1996 when a grant of £130,000 from the Lottery Fund enabled the building of a long-hoped-for new kitchen and scullery and a foyer and green room for the Peter Morrison Recital Hall.

Seventieth Anniversary

On 3 May 1999 a service was held in St Mary's church, Hitchin, to celebrate the 70th Anniversary of the Founding of the Rural Music Schools Association. In his sermon, Canon Michael McAdam spoke first of Mary Ibberson's original vision and continued, 'What the Rural Music Schools Association started the Benslow Music Trust has furthered... Music in our schools today is of a totally different order. But still the vision counts. And so does the enthusiasm. The Benslow schedule of courses for 1999 is breathtaking in its scope. Viol Concerts to Jazz Guitar, Wind Chamber Music to Big Band, Harp to Banjo, lots of singing and much else. All interests, all tastes,all standards catered for and scarcely less important – the instrument loan scheme to put paid to soapbox fiddles.'

Why so Keen to Help?

I probably went non-resident to one weekend course a year at Benslow from the reopening to the late 1980s, when the frequency got better. I was sufficiently committed to the Benslow Music Trust to help with fundraising and join in two events with friends: on July 7th 1989 we raised £200 with a sponsored Beethoven play-in and on the weekend of October 26th to 28th, 1990 we made £1,000 with the Mozart 'Famous Ten.'

Why was I so keen to help? I recognised that without the RMSA and the Benslow Music Trust, and Arnold Ashby, I might not have become a chamber music player and might not have enjoyed orchestra enough to work so hard at being a 'cellist. Benslow was not the only influence – I did play with local groups and do a summer school, but Benslow was the first and consistent resource.

Anne Conchie

Penelope Cave, tutor on the Harpsichord Weekend, 1998.

Trombomania course, 1994.

Glad I Pushed the Boat Out

I first heard about Benslow about ten years ago, probably from a leaflet at Barnet Choral Society. My first visit was to a supper followed by a lecture by Lady Barbirolli on the Friday night, then a stopover and breakfast. I thought I'd treat myself as it sounded a nice break, but money was tight and I had to push the boat out and increase my Barclaycard limit. I had a link with Lady Barbirolli because she was a friend of my harpsichord teacher when I was a teenager. I arrived late and missed supper, but was in time for the lecture on Vaughan Williams. It was very, very good. I was wooed and fell in love with the ambience, it was nice and relaxed, pleasant and casual. No-one stood on ceremony, people made you welcome. It was somewhere a woman on her own could come, it didn't matter that I didn't know anyone. People had

this common interest of music, which focussed the event. That weekend was a springboard. I picked up leaflets, got hooked and came back many times. Benslow often saved my sanity when I was teaching full-time. I felt spiritually refreshed.

I met my husband in December 1992 on an Early Music weekend, so I blessed the day I increased my Barclaycard limit. We have come here together since then, although he sometimes comes alone to the Baroque Orchestra. We like it when there are two courses together, so that after two nights we can get together and perform to each other – lovely. We can share each other's interests and come across new things, such as Barbershop. It broadens our interests.

The leaders are always of a very high standard, first class. Obviously their personalities vary, but you definitely get the best here. Some leaders have a following, for instance we go on a week's course with Stephen Wilkinson every year. Benslow has helped my sight reading and I now do more copying. I am a member of the BBC Symphony Chorus, although really a pianist. I have introduced others, too. Once I brought the whole Barnet Madrigal Society, with Ashley Stafford, in 1990 or '91.

The setting, the atmosphere and the grounds are important. Big windows with plenty of light and the proportions of the rooms are conducive to the magic. When I first came here it was winter and there was a log fire. It is very homely and the staff are caring. There would be a gap in our lives without it. It's so awful driving away, especially after a week's course, almost in tears. It is more like a country house weekend, there's something about it that doesn't exist anywhere else. The combination of music and everything else makes it a unique experience. It brings music

to a lot of people without being ostentatious or patronising. I feel I could stand up at mealtimes and speak as if at a Quaker meeting.

Norma Gillott-King

The Place Just Takes You Over

I came to Benslow in 1989 as a receptionist/clerk. I just wanted a job, but it didn't take me very long to realise that Benslow is not just a job, you either love it or hate it. The house and the place just take you over. It can be stressful but it has a special atmosphere – it is really full of love. I know this because, however unhappy I was at one time, as soon as I entered the house everything changed. Benslow seemed my life – there is a feeling of calm and love in the house. I am

Late night jam session, September 1993.

sure that in bygone days it was very happy. I know other people who have found it a refuge – almost like a religious feeling, like peace in a church.

One old lady used to save up, bring all her own food and stay in one of the rooms in the out-buildings and play the piano to her heart's content. She lived in central London and this was her retreat. I didn't know any history until last year. I look out now and I can imagine croquet on the lawn and the children of the house running about in the woods. This house paints pictures all the time.

My job now is receptionist and clerical administration. I try always to give a personal approach because I am in the forefront, welcoming people. One chap came from Guernsey once and when he went back he sent me an article he had written for a Guernsey newspaper. I was cross because he said that the house welcomes you and the person who opens the door is exactly like Mum all over again. I rang him and he said, 'I'm sorry, Sylv. but that's how we all feel.' Sometimes people come down to breakfast in dressing gown and slippers, they feel at home – that is what I like.

Sylvia Norman

Saxophone Experience, 9 February 1996.

1997, liaising with the Hitchin Museum, the Hitchin Historical Society and the artist Carole Aston, Joan put together an attractive and informative pamphlet, *The Story of Little Benslow Hills* which provides visitors with a helpful introduction.

'The Story of Little Benslow Hills'

Joan Jelliffe, a violin and viola player, began coming to Benslow, for string course weekends, in 1965. A member of Council since 1979, she became aware over the years that few of the continuous stream of visitors knew anything of the history of the house. Examination candidates and their parents, in particular, often enquired for a guide-book, but nothing was available. In

CHAPTER 9

The Musical Instrument Loan Scheme

The Joachim Quartet, 1890s. (1st violin: Joachim, 2nd violin: -?-, viola: Wirth, 'cello: Hausman). Both Editha Knocker and Phyllis Eyre studied with Joachim.

Editha Knocker

Editha Knocker was born on 2 March 1868 in Devonshire, into a Quaker family. Little is known of her childhood. She studied from 1886 to 1891 with Joachim in Berlin and became leader of his students' orchestra – this caused a lot of jealousy among the other players – for a woman to be leader was unthinkable at the time.

When Editha Knocker was unable to continue her career as a performer due to neuritis in her arm she was invited to join the famous violinist Leopold Auer as his assistant at the Conservatoire of St Petersburg. He taught Mischa Elman, Jascha Heifetz, Efrem Zimbalist and many other virtuoso violinists. It was this experience with the brilliant young players of the time that helped to make her such a remarkable teacher. She returned to England on the outbreak of war in 1914.

I was one of of Editha Knocker's pupils. I won the Director's Scholarship to her School of Violin Playing at 67, Finchley Road, Hampstead, a beautiful Regency house now, alas, pulled down. It was small, rather like the Menuhin School, specialising in violin, viola and chamber music and training the students for a performing career. She was very choosy about her pupils.

It was a great privilege to be taught by Editha Knocker. I believe she taught at the Mount School in York, then at the Royal Academy of Music for about a year. Everyone there wanted to be taught by her and so she was not very popular with the other staff. Her friend Mrs Croll, a very rich widow, gave her the financial support to begin her school. Mrs Croll and Urik Tschaikovsky were co-directors. She insisted that the teaching staff must use fine instruments, so that students were accustomed from the beginning to hear a beautiful sound. She tried to get them good instruments as well.

One of her lasting memorials is the Loan Scheme, originally called the Editha Knocker Violin Loan Scheme. She conceived the idea and with great generosity Mrs Croll financed it and organised it from her house in Frognal, Hampstead. It continues as the Benslow Violin Loan Scheme.

Phyllis Ebsworth

Good Violins Lying Idle

Sir,
May we bring to the notice of music lovers everywhere, through your columns, a scheme which, while involving no expense to those participating, would be of incalculable value to violin and viola students all over the country?

All those familiar with the teaching of music are aware of the difficulties experienced by advanced students in purchasing adequate instruments, and of the discouragement caused in consequence. There must be many good violins and violas lying idle and unused in homes throughout the country, whose owners, for sentimental or other reasons, have no wish to sell them, but who would be glad to lend them to serious students. The loan would benefit both owner and student, for string instruments do not improve by lying idle. It is proposed that such string instruments should be lent, under the advice of responsible teachers, to promising pupils for the purpose of study and public performance, we, the undersigned taking full responsibility for their care and covering them against all risks by insurance. Messrs W.E. Hill and Sons, of 140, New Bond Street, the well-known violin experts,

Editha Knocker.

have kindly consented to advise upon the value, for insurance purposes, of each instrument.

The outlines of the scheme have been submitted to and approved by: Sir Hugh Allen, Sir Walford Davies, Sir Henry Hadow, Sir John McEwen, Sir Landon Ronald, Sir Robert Witt, Sir Henry Wood, Mrs Newmarch, Mr Samuel Courtauld, Professor E.J. Dent, Mr Robert Mayer, Mr Herbert Wiseman and Mr W.W. Cobbett.

All those who are willing to help in the interests of national music by the loan of violins and violas are requested to communicate with Mrs George Croll, 9, Westbourne Street, W2 from whom further particulars can be obtained.

Yours truly,
Editha G. Knocker
Edith G. Croll

Letter in the Times,
Saturday January 23rd 1932

Immediate Response

The letter in the *Times* brought an immediate response. A typical reply came from a Mrs Anley, who explained to Mrs Croll that she had lost her husband and her children and had no-one to whom to leave her violin. She wished to find it a good home, where it would be used and she offered to deliver it in person. From this initial contact a long and friendly correspondence followed, which must have given some consolation to the lonely widow. The time and individual care which both Editha Knocker and Mrs Croll gave to those who loaned or donated instruments is quite remarkable. Not for them the impersonal efficiency of printed receipts or stereotyped letters: every communication received a personal reply, often handwritten. The correspondence relating to each instrument was meticulously filed, along with printed cards on which borrowers were asked to 'Report, please on condition of — .' Sometimes the Loan Scheme had the effect of renewing old friendships:

A Pupil from 40 Years Ago

Jan. 24th 1932
Dear Miss Knocker,
Having seen the letter in yesterday's Times I am hastening to send the viola which I tried to play with your help forty years ago! and shall be glad to hear whether you can find a home for it or use it yourself. It was bought for me… in Leeds about 1890! for £15 and I fear it will have suffered from lack of using – 'tho I have lent it to friends from time to time. Of course I do not want anything for it – (unless you should care to sell for the Musicians' Benevolent Society). I am also sending the little book you took so much trouble to write and illustrate for me – do you ever come to York now? or is your headquarters in London? I know that you made a living? and successful 'career' and that you have also taken a leading part adjudicating at Musical Competition Festivals.
And I have been busy looking after a family.
With my kind remembrances,

Yours sincerely,
Evelyn Peake (once Dundas)

I Remember Your Viola's Face

25/1/32
Dear Mrs Peake,
It was delightful to have your letter and to find

The Ebsworth String Quarter, c. 1945. Left to right: Eileen Ebsworth, Elizabeth Hunt, Phyllis Ebsworth, Eleanor Warren.

that old friends are not forgotten. It gives one quite a shock when a pupil announces that she had lessons forty years ago! What a grandmother I have become!

I seem to remember your viola's face quite well, but shall see when it arrives whether this is fancy only. I shall be very glad to have the use of it for my youngsters, and shall see that it is looked after well, you may be sure…

I live entirely in London, since 1916, and only travel about when judging or lecturing. Thank you too for sending me the little book which was written while I was still a student in Berlin. That must be at least forty three years ago! I should be sorry to attempt those drawings now, though I think I might do something better

from the literary point of view!
With kindest remembrances,

yours sincerely,
Editha Knocker

The Ezra Pound Connection

An intriguing little sidelight was shed on literary history by a correspondence between Editha Knocker and Dorothy Pound, wife of the American Imagist poet, Ezra Pound. Mrs Pound had offered a 'cello for the Loan Scheme, but a planned meeting had had to be put off because Editha

Knocker was unwell. On 27 September 1937, Mrs Pound wrote to say that she regretted not being able to see Miss Knocker and suggested that she might like to have tea with her mother, who would be 'delighted to give you tea and show you the 'cello.' Mrs Pound herself hoped 'to be leaving for Rapallo on Friday 1st.' Two years later, a card, postmarked 'Rapallo, Italy, 24/7/39' reached Mrs Croll at her Scottish address, with the message, 'So glad to think the 'cello is being so useful and appreciated. Hoping to meet again "some day"... Dorothy Pound'. A note on the loan scheme record card says tersely, 'Unable to report owing to war conditions,' but when the upheavals of war were over, contact was re-established and the loan allowed to continue for many years.

Louis Carus

In 1936, at the age of eight, Louis Carus borrowed, from the Scheme, a fine three-quarter size old German violin. Louis' mother, a professional pianist, knew about the Scheme and she contacted Edith Croll, explaining that Louis was using a violin that was not bringing enough sound to his level of playing. Edith Croll herself brought the instrument to Folkestone, where Louis' father was an education officer at the nearby Shorncliffe army camp.

Even Practising Was Fun

The violin made an immediate difference. Before, I was playing with a basic, factory-made instrument. Suddenly, with the Loan Scheme violin, I was playing like I had never played before. Even practising was fun. The sound I was making was so much stronger that I was asked to play in local festivals and it marked the beginning of my career. At ten years old, I was heartbroken when I grew out of it and my parents bought me a full-size instrument.

Louis Carus

New Trustees

After Editha Knocker's death in 1950, Mrs Croll continued the Loan Scheme, but inevitably the time came when she felt it necessary to hand on what had become a considerable workload to others. By 1960 the Loan Scheme was responsible for 108 instruments, nearly all violins, but also a few violas and 'cellos and on 1 March that year a Trust Deed was signed between Mrs Croll and the new trustees, Desmond D'Artrey Hill, the violin maker and Jean Hadley (formerly Jean Stewart, viola of the Isolde Menges Quartet).

The RMSA and the Loan Scheme

In May 1984, the RMSA was approached by the trustees of the Violin Loan Scheme, who were now seeking new trustees to take over from them. The Scheme had accumulated, we were told, some hundreds of instruments, most of which it owned, while some were loaned to it by their owners. The Scheme also had substantial financial reserves. The sum of £80,000 was mentioned.

This news was given to the RMSA Executive Committee. Two members, John Myatt and I, were keenly in favour of taking on the Scheme. The treasurer said we did not want the responsibility. Others were interested more in the cash reserves than anything else. We agreed that we would be interested to know more, and that the Director should consult our solicitor.

The RMSA's interest in the VLS continued to be dominated by the view 'that £70,000 would be made available to RMSA – it was felt that this could legitimately be used for development work' – which meant, for the proposed conversion of the coach-house to a studio and bedrooms. John Myatt and I opposed this view. We urged that RMSA should adopt the VLS, and run it as its founders had intended. It would, we said, benefit the RMSA by widening its charitable purposes. In September a letter from the VLS trustees referred to 'an element of misunderstanding'. The transfer was now in doubt.

By December the VLS trustees had 'responded negatively to the suggestion that they should meet the chairman of the RMSA.' The treasurer reported 'disappointment over the VLS'. John Myatt and I had seen a story in the Sunday Times about two talented young brothers, a violinist and a 'cellist, in desperate need of good instruments. We urged that the RMSA should tell the VLS trustees that we wanted to offer, via the Sunday Times, to supply such instruments. And already an elderly friend of mine was interested in lending several 'cellos to the Scheme. John Myatt said he knew Desmond Hill and offered to contact him. John and I together worked out an approach to Mr Hill, to bring in the Sunday Times story, and the offer of 'cellos. We thought that if he could bring Mr Hill round, and if the Scheme came to RMSA, our trustees would, for a start, write to the Sunday Times.

In January 1985 we heard that the VLS trustees had 'after all' agreed to transfer the Scheme to us. The deed transferring the VLS was signed in April – eleven months after the first approach. John Myatt produced a paper, 'The VLS: a personal view' urging adoption of

a policy of 'positive growth' and reminding us that he had told Desmond Hill that that was what we would do.

At the Council meeting in October a subcommittee was appointed to 'sit with' the VLS trustees; including John Myatt and me.

Richard Wiggs

Launch Event

Talented young musicians in North Herts. get a helping hand from Benslow Music Trust in Hitchin with the launch of a new instrument loan scheme.

The scheme, which gets underway this month will help to provide better instruments for youngsters in schools and colleges throughout the area.

At the launch on Sunday there will be an exhibition of old and new instruments owned or acquired by the Trust, a demonstration of new instruments by the celebrated Alberni String Quartet, a TV film about the Quartet finishing with a supper and comments by Chairman of the Loan Scheme Governors, David Moore.

The North Herts Gazette, 14 November 1987

The Caring Face of Benslow

I am not very musical but I like listening to music. When I retired I asked if there was anything I could do. I began by being chairman of the Loan Scheme Ten Year Anniversary and stayed with it. I do lots of basic things like transporting instruments or going to concerts and taking displays. When I meet professional musicians and talk about Benslow, they tend to say, 'Oh yes, the Loan Scheme,' rather than the other work. Someone said, 'Is this the caring face of Benslow?'

Recently the Sorrell Quartet came to Benslow and ran a course. The viola player, Vicki Wardman, had actually borrowed an instrument from us and she is now teaching a student who has also borrowed one of our instruments.

Anne Parker

A Distinguished Career

Louis Carus has had a distinguished career in music. He was a music scholar at Rugby School and later studied at the Brussels Conservatoire with Dubois and Grumiaux. He completed his studies at Peabody Conservatory in Baltimore, USA. In 1950 he joined the Scottish National Orchestra and in 1955 he became Head of the string Department at the Royal Scottish Academy of Music and drama. In 1975 he became Principal and Dean of Faculty of the Birmingham School of Music (now Birmingham Conservatoire) where he founded the Granville Ensemble, and was deeply involved with the development of the school graduate courses and buildings, including the Adrian Boult hall.

Since 1987 Louis Carus has been an invaluable help to the Loan Scheme. He has been the main force in building up the Scheme to a national presence from one hundred instruments to its present number of nearly five hundred. He reviews every instrument that comes into the scheme to assess its condition and its level of suitability for borrowers, and he sees every instrument that is returned from loan to make sure that it has been well maintained. More recently, during 1998 and 1999 he has personally organised and financed nearly a dozen concerts for the benefit of the Scheme and arranged for prestigious musicians to play

at them. The growth of the Scheme and its many friends and donors is due mainly to Louis Carus. His energy and concern seem to come from his own personal experience of the loan of an instrument: he has certainly given back a hundredfold the help he once received from the Scheme.

Benslow Loan Scheme Newsletter,
Autumn 1999

I Felt Like a Broker's man

I just didn't realise how much an instrument deteriorates if left unplayed. For example, there was a widow whose husband wanted three instruments to come to Benslow, but she held on to them for about ten years for sentiment. When she contacted me I went down and collected them (I felt like a broker's man, taking away part of their history). One instrument was valued at over £2,000 and needed work doing. We spent about £700 on it and it was then re-valued at £7,000. It is now one of our most valuable and important violas. When people loan an instrument we keep them very involved with what's happening. When they give it, we write and thank them, but it is not possible to do much more.

Anne Parker

The Aims of Today's Scheme

* To seek out promising young players at any stage of their musical education who, in order to advance, need a better instrument than they can afford.
* To appeal for and search out under-used instruments, and to rescue unused instruments from confinement in cupboards, to set them in order and get them into the hands of needy

young musicians.
* To keep costs and formalities to the minimum consistent with efficiency and good stewardship.

Loan Scheme brochure

The Borrowers

The Scheme tries to give precedence to students who could not otherwise afford to buy or hire. Borrowers are charged a deposit, but this is made as affordable as possible. Most people hear about the scheme from teachers or lecturers. Adults are not usually accepted, but there are exceptions, such as one borrower who was introduced to music as a therapy following illness and was found to have an aptitude for it. There are Loan Scheme borrowers in every part of the United Kingdom, including students at all the leading conservatoires, at the Yehudi Menuhin School, the Purcell School, Chethams School and Wells Cathedral School.

Looking After Instruments

The Scheme's largest expense is the cost of repairs, currently in the region of £45,000 per year, mainly the result of wear and tear. Sometimes donated instruments arrive needing a great deal of restoration work. Loaned instruments are usually repaired by their owners. Instruments are insured by British Reserve who are specialists in this field. New instruments are insured for replacement value, old instruments for what it is assumed they will fetch at auction. It is very rare for the Scheme to face the total loss of an instrument. Most insurance claims are for accidental damage, perhaps ten per year, out of 500 instruments and usually for quite small things. Borrowers are given careful guidance on how to look after their instruments.

Tenth Anniversary

In 1995 it was felt that we ought to celebrate the tenth anniversary of the Benslow administration of the Scheme. We asked people who had borrowed instruments to play for us and we had an extraordinary time. Concerts were given for us by the Alberni Quartet at St James, Piccadilly, by Wells Cathedral School, the Purcell School, the Yehudi Menuhin School and by others at Birmingham, Manchester, Glasgow. They brought a lot of publicity and the number of instruments in the Scheme almost doubled.

Anne Parker

Buying Instruments

The Loan Scheme occasionally buys instruments. In 1998 it bought a collection of instruments on show at the Royal College of Music. There is also a local trust, the Evelyn Wrightson Memorial Trust at Much Hadham, which set aside money to buy musical instruments and gave two thirds of their capital to the Loan Scheme. The instruments which were bought with this money have given a welcome boost to the collection. A small number of instruments have been bought through a sponsorship arrangement, whereby the Loan Scheme pays half and individuals or a small trust, such as the Bulldog Trust in London, pay the other half.

Violin practice. (Courtesy Simon Baker)

A Child's Progress

A child might start learning at school with a Chinese Stentor instrument for about £100, or an eastern European one costing a little more. For a full-size violin, which a child can play from about eleven to twelves years old, a reasonable instrument costs from about £700 to £1000. A child who does well will soon need a better one. It is also good for children to get the feel of a variety of instruments. Several borrowers who have tried instruments by one of our modern makers often go direct to the maker when they can afford one. The most expensive instruments in the Scheme are valued at about £45,000 but that is not expensive. Stringed instruments played by professionals

would be valued in six figures. Players do not usually own them but have them on loan from private sponsors, trusts or a music college.

Min Jin Kim

When the talented young violinist Min Jin Kim, was at the Purcell School she had the use of the scheme's Panormo violin (on loan to us from the Sefton family). This violin, made by the Italian craftsman Vincenzo Panormo, who died in 1813, originally belonged to Dorothy Churton, a pupil of Karl Flesch, who purchased it from Panormo. The instrument has remained in the same family through the generations and was loaned to the Scheme by the Sefton family in 1988. Min Jin has been invited to perform as a soloist with the Philharmonia Orchestra in the 1999/2000 and 2000/20001 seasons, with concerts at major British regional venues leading to her Royal Festival Hall debut in the autumn of 2000.

Loan Scheme brochure

The Key that Sets Them off

Although the idea behind the Loan Scheme is simple and straightforward, its administration is time-consuming. The task of keeping track of instruments and borrowers has been streamlined with the computerisation of records, but much depends on the dedication of the Scheme's staff. One said, 'The thing I enjoy most of all is seeing the faces of youngsters when they play a really good instrument for the first time. Often parents ring a few days later and tell us that their child hasn't stopped practising. It is the key that sets them off.'

CHAPTER 10

Planning for a New Millennium

Rehearsal in bedroom, 1998. (Courtesy Howard Davis).

Charm of the old house

For many people, the excellent tuition, the joy of music-making with fellow-enthusiasts and the charm of Little Benslow Hills itself, outweighed the inconveniences of staying in far from purpose-built accommodation. Good-humouredly the majority of students – most of whom were of fairly mature years – accepted the need to share rooms, or to turn their bedrooms into practice rooms. The staff

did their best to meet individual requirements, but this could mean an uneconomic use of space, if, for example, a large room with several beds was allocated to one person. Sometimes it proved impossible to allocate suitable rooms at Benslow and students were offered accommodation in the homes of nearby residents, who had generously agreed to help in this way. Matching this assortment of rooms with the needs of students was not easy for the staff but, with much goodwill from all concerned, it worked surprising well for many years. Towards the end of the 1990s, comments in the Benslow Visitors' Book, although still overwhelmingly enthusiastic (approximately 88% favourable between 1995 and 1997), are increasingly outspoken about the shortcomings of their accommodation.

Heaven – or Hell on Earth?

'*A stimulating and educational experience in delightful surroundings enhanced by the company of the musicians and the opportunities to paint them, converse with them and enjoy their concert. The Seebohms would be delighted to know the excellent and constructive use to which their home has been put and the hospitality and comfort provided by those who so efficiently and modestly administer the Trust.*'

'*This must be the nearest place to Heaven that we'll find on this earth. Thanks a lot.*'

'*Thanks to Betty for the marvellous coaching! Congratulations to the gardener and to the librarians for the excellent state of the garden and library, and to the staff in general for their kindness and efficiency. Do remember for the future: "Small is beautiful".*'

'*As always it was a wonderful time. Splendid working with the tutors as well. I enjoyed the room in the Lodge, but it is a little difficult for a very small person, in mid 70s, to get the 'cello, in hard case, up and down the stairs. The weight of the 'cello pulls one downstairs. Perhaps extend the information on age to include '70 plus?'*

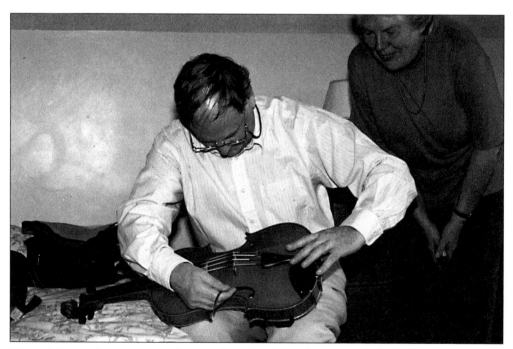

Howard Davis adjusting the soundpost on Louise's viola in Spring-Rice bedroom, where four people were practising and having tutorials, 1998.

'Sunday. The sleep of the unfortunate resident of Purcell is governed by visits made to the two toilets (one each side), early morning baths, use of the tea station and noises off – also creaking floor boards from above. This room is a HELL HOLE. After very little sleep I now have to drive 140 miles. The David Ball Course is excellent – and I don't like to complain – but sleep is essential if one is to take full advantages of all that is offered.

Comments from the 1995-97 Benslow Visitors' Book

The National Lottery

From early in the 1990s it seemed to us that long term plans to improve the buildings and facilities at Benslow needed to be made. We undertook detailed research within our membership, but gave the assurance that the overall scale of Benslow, and its comfortable intimacy would not be lost.

Our argument was that Benslow could not justify its claims to providing a unique home for amateur music making if bedrooms had to be vacated for playing, if plumbing was antique, the kitchen almost impenetrable, the pianos poor and so on. The stark economic facts also became clear – Benslow's work would remain unviable unless future facilities allowed the average attendance at weekend courses to rise from twenty-plus to much nearer forty people. This would depend absolutely on better quality accommodation, with many more single bedrooms, better social facilities and a dramatic improvement in the music making environment. We also knew that we must take into account the needs of the disabled and disadvantaged: putting up attendance fees was not the answer.

With the advent of the Lottery in 1995 we were amongst the first to advance all these arguments in a formal application. It was an immense, detailed task, which we undertook ourselves with much volunteer help, and with advice from the authorities concerned. We paid a modest fee to Barry Dickens, our architect, for him to work up our sketch brief and obtain planning permission for a new block across the most neglected stretch of our car park, the former kitchen gardens. It should all have cost about £400,000 and would have done us proud. We asked the Lottery to assess it and applied for their maximum grant, 75% of total costs. Our application went through the due processes, we were visited and quizzed – even grilled – by a range of supportive people. Then we sat and waited for the result.

David Moore

A Missed opportunity

In December 1995, the result of the Lottery application was received. It offered an immediate grant of £140,000 towards the costs of essential renovations and improvements to the Victorian building. Most of this money was spent on a complete modernisation programme for the kitchens.

However, the application for the planned extension was rejected and its design criticised as a missed opportunity to achieve something architecturally outstanding, even though it would adequately have met Benslow's needs. But the Trust was encouraged to reapply, subject to the appointment of another architect, chosen from a small number recommended by the Arts Council itself. The Benslow proposals had been accepted in principle and the range and quality of its work endorsed and acclaimed.

No Concessions to the Past

During 1996 we accepted the Arts Council's advice, and appointed Patel Taylor, of Camden, London as our Architects. This time there would be no concession to our Victorian past; for the first time we were fully exposed to outside streams of thought, and also more conscious that we would not be free to insist, as clients, on our own point of view.

The new design took shape over the following months. In content it fully met the needs of our brief, providing a second rehearsal hall, four playing rooms for smaller groups, and six bedrooms on the first floor, two of which can accommodate the disabled, all with en-suite facilities, thus beginning the process of increasing the number of single rooms at Benslow and meeting the demand for private bathrooms. However, in concept the design is much more ambitious in its enclosure of a new courtyard, which will eventually be the largest of three linked open spaces around which the music activity will take place, shifting the musical focus of Benslow away from the Victorian house, and requiring many parts of the other buildings to be upgraded. When re-submitted to the Arts Council for assessment the design received very high praise, outweighing our own reservations about the provision of a flat roof and choice of some other materials.

David Moore

Fund-raising

When the new application was submitted, it was in the hope that the money which the Benslow Music Trust would be required to raise itself would not exceed £150,000. In the event, after five years of development and fund-raising, it raised over £400,000 towards building costs which will total in excess of £1,500,000. This was made possible by the support of the membership, the help of many Trusts and the generosity of a small number of long term friends who bequeathed money to Benslow.

In 1998, after the Arts Council had made a further award of £975,000, and all the details of design and planning formalities had been completed, a contract was signed for the new building, which began in January 1999, for intended completion in November. A celebration weekend had been planned for just before Christmas, but delays crept in and began to accumulate, so that completion of the building is now anticipated for mid-2000. The building process was not easy: the design proved exceptionally complex, with many bespoke features, and in 1999 other millennium projects throughout the country were also competing for materials and labour to meet their Year 2000 deadlines.

As the new buildings were nearing completion, Benslow received two enormously generous and unexpected legacies, the first, in 1999, from Edwina Palmer and the second, in March 2000, from Dorothea Waldeck. The names of these two benefactors will be kept alive for future generations in the 'Waldeck Buildings' and the 'Edwina Palmer Hall'.

A Place for Art

The Lottery grant from the Arts Council requires us to adopt a wide range of policies to achieve local usage, accessibility and equal opportunities, all of which will require active future management on our part. The capital programme must provide 1% expenditure for art. In our case this has taken the form of a competition by selective tender for a sculpture beside the pool in the new courtyard, for which Christine Fox was selected. In addition Benslow is creating a bursary in conjunction with the Arts Council for North Hertfordshire, to allow an artist or craftsman from the region to have an annual loan exhibition in the foyer.

David Moore

The Old and the new

The new buildings are not an end in themselves. Many people have attended and loved the 'old' Benslow, some for fifty years or longer, but few deny the necessity of change. The Lottery has voted money for this change. Of the £1,500,000 planned to be spent, in one way or another nearly one quarter will provide improvements to existing facilities – although

The curved foyer of the Waldeck Buildings nearing completion, May 2000.

The Edwina Palmer Hall, May 2000.

many items have to be delayed until we can bring the new buildings themselves into use – otherwise the running of the Course Programme would be interrupted.

Thus Benslow is likely to remain a building site, in some degree, until well into 2001. The domestic and catering scene at Benslow has long struggled with cramped facilities, and the arrival of a new kitchen has only accented the inadequacy of the dining room and other social amenities.

Provided that expenditure overall does not overrun, we expect to extend the present dining room into the bar, and to link the main house with the Recital Hall, providing a new bar and social facilities within that link, together with the facility, at present missing, for wheel chairs to move around the the whole group of buildings, old and new, without confronting steps.

David Moore

Justifiably Proud

Throughout the past five years, we have sought the views of our membership – well over one thousand individuals and families who form the backbone and security for our work – in all that has been done at Benslow. Without their backing and their generous financial support none of this could have been undertaken. Surprisingly only a tiny number have voiced concern at the degree of change. It is very unlikely that such a spurt of capital investment in buildings will ever take place again. It is astonishing that it has been carried through so successfully and with such little disturbance to the making of music.

In the short term the priorities will now shift to utilising the new facilities to the full, for which we will need to gather together many new, and younger friends. We are also seeking Lottery support to expand our Instrument Loan Scheme and we at last have the chance to consider how we can broaden the scope of the Benslow Music Trust, reaching out to others in the spirit of Esther Seebohm's bequest to us.

The head count of all those who have been consulted during the past years – Arts Council personnel, architects, surveyors, engineers of many disciplines, local government and specialist consultants – number well over 100. They cannot all be formally listed in the 'cast list' which follows, indeed there may be many of whom we do not even know, but we hope they all count amongst our friends.

David Moore

Edwina Palmer

Edwina Palmer died in 1999, just before her 104th birthday, in a Seaford nursing home. She had heard from Yehudi Menuhin for her 100th

---

The Arts Council of England provided lottery funds in 1998-2000 towards total capital costs of £1,500,000 for the design and construction of new facilities at Benslow. The following firms and individuals were directly concerned in the project:

Architect:
Patel Taylor (Andrew Taylor, Pankaj Patel, Adam Penton and Tim Riley)

Quantity Surveyor:
Dearle & Henderson (Peter Hancock, Peter Gudge and Darren Kaley)

Services Engineer:
Ove Arup & Partners (Phil Nedin, Simon Luff and Daymon Brocklebank)

Acoustic Engineer:
Arup Acoustics (Raf Orlowski)

Structural Engineer:
Alan Conisbee & Associates (Tim Attwood and Ian Prentice)

Contractor:
C. Miskin & Sons Limited

Arts Council Monitor: John Mason
Courtyard Sculpture: Christine Fox
Period Furnishings: Phoenix Restorations
Furniture: Tract Limited

Project Manager for Benslow Music Trust:
Richard Moore

Development Fund-Raising and Membership Committees:
David Moore, Owen Stable, Stephen Cooper, David Thorpe, Tony Aston, Graham Felton, Ruth Maguire, Monica Moore, Nicolas Wickham-Irving, Michael Willoughby, Michael Taylor.

Secretary to the Committees: Jane Jenkins

birthday. Isolde Menges gave Edwina much joy on that occasion by playing her first violin solo amongst other items played by a group of Edwina's former students. It was fitting that Isolde played Massenet's 'Meditation' at Edwina's requiem mass four years later, with a good number of her former pupils present. It is wonderful that the new hall at Benslow is to be named after her.

Elizabeth Black (nee Mason)

The New Hall

Now the new building is all but finished. It is even difficult to remember what was there before, or to imagine how such a large cuckoo squeezed into this position so close to its Victorian parent. To the chance visitor, strolling up Benslow Lane and glancing casually towards Little Benslow Hills, the unexpected glare of a new white wall comes as a shock. Not until the exterior is seen in its entirety, the circular wall of the concert hall and the paved area, with its pool, linking the old and new buildings, is it possible to begin to appreciate the architect's intentions.

Inside, the building is a revelation – quite beautiful in its combination of high quality, traditional materials and a modern design which manages to be both exciting and restful. On entering the foyer, a curved space well-illuminated and with a cleverly-integrated display area, the visitor is at once entranced by the lightness, the illusion of space and the pleasing proportions. The concert hall is visually a delight, even if the quirkiness of its ceiling design makes replacing light-bulbs an unusually hi-tech feat.

On the ground-floor are practice-rooms designed to be soundproof and upstairs, compact, well-appointed study bedrooms with an attractive – but rather unusual – window ventilation feature. Soon the building will come alive to the sound of music and laughter and a whole new set of Benslow traditions will evolve within it.

The Waldeck Buildings, May 2000.

CHAPTER 11

A Spirit of Making Music

Jen Lynch, 1998. (Courtesy Howard Davis)

A Day at Benslow Music Trust

Ring the bell, struggle with the front door and enter a dim hall-way, where a solitary figure is sitting, reading peacefully on one of the two large, soft settees. A standard lamp illuminates the display of goods for sale, including 'organic apples, handpicked.' On a small table a new violin is displayed, brought by from the other side of England by the craftsman who made it. There is a pleasant aroma of coffee. In the bar, Chinese lanterns and honesty decorate the hearth, there are fresh flowers on the mantelpiece. It is break-time for today's course members, a string sextet. They are happy, a little excitable, pleased to talk.

The Joy of Chamber Music

Chamber music is so rewarding. The joy of being a team member is really great when four of you are playing well and you know you are

String quartet, left to right: Pat Stove, Louise Stewart-Cox, Anne Conchie, Janet Tanner (leader).

Matthew Souter, viola player with the Alberni Quartet, conducting a class, 1998. (Courtesy Howard Davis).

playing well and can enjoy each other's achievements. It is a joy I haven't found anywhere else. I can't imagine life without being a 'cellist and it's a bad day if I don't practice. My friends are in music: if you took music away I would have difficulty. I would have to completely rebuild my life.

Anne Conchie

The Instrument Maker

There are quite a lot of instrument makers now, not only in Britain, but internationally, and many travel to work abroad. At the moment, for instance, it seems that there are as many Germans working in London, making and repairing, as there are British people. Equally when I worked in Germany there were repairers from five different countries in the workshop.

I come to Benslow about five or six times a year because they run so many chamber courses. The staff are helpful and friendly and the atmosphere is relaxed, which suits me. People have come to enjoy themselves and there is time for them to talk to me and play my instruments. Often they have queries about their own instruments and I can usually find the problem and suggest a remedy. Talking to the tutors and hearing them play my instruments is also very useful for me in assessing my work.

I play a bit, enough to start the instruments off and get a good idea of how they're working and after that I take them to the best musician I can find before I make the final adjustments. There is about six weeks of work in a violin or viola, but varnish needs time to dry, so I start work on the next while the first is drying. Although I do make instruments to order, I prefer to make an instrument and then find a buyer, as it gives me more freedom.

My visits to Benslow I see as promotional work. A good 90% of players are happy with the instrument they've got, so I don't sell an instrument every time I come. But maybe a month or so later I get a call from somebody wanting to try an instrument. So it is worth it.

William Castle

I am Glad I Came

England has had a long period of amateur music making for various social reasons. It is the way things developed here, where amateur music is rather more popular than in other countries. You can be a complete beginner and come to Benslow and it's all right. In the atmosphere a certain feeling of 'Easy.' This last course included a number of people who hadn't been before, some good players, some not – but all enjoy themselves and it does not matter.

We never seemed to attract quite young people, but it doesn't matter; young people get a lot of help but older people need it too. We do foundation courses and the standard is mixed. Often people haven't played in quartets and this gives them the opportunity. You can have quartets at different levels in different rooms, they don't impede each other. In chamber music you are responsible for your own part, in an orchestra you can tag along.

I am very glad I came to Hitchin and to Benslow. Here I am at this advanced age and I can't imagine anything else being so good. I am deaf, but I can hear music: speech depends on consonants, but that is not so in music. For old people it is nice to go on being active and useful.

Anne Macnaghten

A Macnaghten summer school. Left to right: Audrey Catford ('cello), Pauline Sekyi and friends. (Courtesy Simon Baker)

A Spirit of Music Making

There is a spirit of making music that just cannot go from Benslow. It's a place that you feel was created out of the right ideals in the beginning, somewhere that people can make music together as amateur musicians, play and be taught and be coached. There is nowhere else like it. People like the Macnaghtens have been here throughout – the thread has never been lost. That's why I'm happy to be on Council still. Although we may drive each other nuts we all feel the same way, we all want to keep it here.

Juliet Abrahamson

Then and Now

It is so different now, the whole ethos. When I was in the Rural Music School we were dealing with people who couldn't afford much – not the people you would find here today. Of course people are not tied to their villages as they were, the majority of people have access to larger towns. Also, until the recent cuts, the government paid for music lessons in schools. When I was teaching in the 1980s, I looked at a Benslow brochure and thought, 'No one here could afford it.'

And there is a bar now, compared with the previous teetotal atmosphere. There is no longer a Quaker ethos. But it is a wonderful place for people to come. Standards are very high – you really are learning all the time and the best got out of you. There are very good teachers. One of my first courses in recent years was a 'sponsored sing' with Michael Procter, of the complete 'Gradualia' of William Byrd. We sang for five hours one day – an incredible experience.

In general the whole standard of music in my

lifetime has changed so completely. The RMS movement has contributed to that. The standard at which people go into a music college course now is about the standard we used to come out at.

Grisell Davies (nee Roy)

Nothing Else Like It

In Mary Ibberson's time there was nothing else like it until the counties took over. It was the only residential school of its kind for amateurs. It has meant a lot to me over the years. I feel part of it. I am too old to go very often (no car now) but there is always a very friendly group working there.

The Christmas parties started with dinner on the first evening. There was an orchestra and a singing group, two sessions in the morning, a session after tea and another after dinner. Next day there were madrigals, then the main conductor would take the choir, then the orchestra with quartets. Then in the evening there was a party. One night would be serious, one night light entertainment and games. It wasn't particularly seasonal music and it was quite hard work! The house was full up last year. Lots of people on their own and some couples.

Doris Gare

Wonderful Things Are Happening

It is very difficult to be objective about Benslow now, because of getting old, regretting change, longing for things to be as you remember them; but I do think there's a danger of going with the

The bar, 1998.

Stephen Wilkinson conducting at his Choral Weekend, 1998.

Dido and Aeneas, 1999.

New Year course, 1995/6. Left to right; Monica Moore, Howard Etherington, -?-.

tide too much. When there were very few staff we had a simplicity, a readiness to muck in where practical things were concerned. It would be awfully sad to be losing that for amenities and facilities. But some things were bad and it is great to have them remedied, for example the coaching in tiny bedrooms. Wonderful things are going on in the music world with children and others with special needs. I can't help feeling that that's something we could move into rather than make it even more convenient and comfortable for people who are really well-established.

There is a huge role for people living on their own. I have been going at Christmas time for some years. We get a lot of people who have rather sad reasons for coming and are seriously lonely. It is a wonderful and very happy time.

Sarah Graham

We Come Here to Do Something

I used to come regularly to courses when Norman had sort of 'family' weekends. We were all friends together, we all knew each other. Then I suggested a course for double bass players. Someone said that nobody would want it but I was determined we should. I got hold of Rodney Slatford and persuaded him to come here and run a course. These went on for about twelve years, and sundry beginners and advanced came. Quite a few are now in the profession. Rodney Slatford is a marvellous teacher.

Music is a thing one does. I'm not a great listener. Benslow is important because there is an enormous number of active amateur musicians and this is the place that provides for them. The emphasis has changed from being a Rural School of Music to what it is now. Most people come here to do something, they don't want just to listen passively. They want to get on and play or sing. When I see an orchestra I'm itching to play in it. I'm now eighty four and can't keep up playing, the instrument is too heavy. I have had an enormous amount of fun – playing in about sixteen major operas, all the major choral works, all the Beethoven symphonies and so on. I started off as a professional and became an amateur. Now I am taking up the piano again.

Robin Miller

It was set up by a middle class enthusiast, but Miss Ibberson nevertheless produced genuine benefits. Our course programme is difficult to sell and each year we have to cancel some. A residential music course is not a very saleable commodity. There must be other things we could do that would be less costly to run, but would benefit a wider range of people who really need 'charitable' assistance.

Richard Wiggs

Genuine Benefits

I think one thing that is wrong is that like so many other charities, historically, it has been high-jacked by the affluent middle classes. It is also a small business.

A Place of Prestige

When I first joined, some prestigious people were asked to help the RMSA, it wasn't a place of local prestige. Now, locally, to be on the Council of Benslow means something.

Orchestral Summer School, 1990s. (Courtesy Keith Stent)

When I was first asked to join I had never heard of it. Rural Music Schools were just places where people could come along of an evening to have violin lessons. To be involved in Benslow now is a prestige matter, especially locally. A few people are attracted to it for self-aggrandisement.

Francis Oakes

Music is My Life

I have a story to tell which has made my life such a joy since my retirement. I was a late starter on the clarinet at fifty years old, learning that finger on that hole means E. Just before retiring I discovered Benslow, and after retirement, at fifty-eight, I have attended several times each year. Various courses and many patient tutors have led me to enjoy wind ensembles of all descriptions.

At home in desperation I held a weekly 'Open House' for clarinettists (for mature, late starters), this was ten years ago and it has gone from strength to strength. I was invaded by a flute player, which made me learn how to transpose. Then an oboist crept in. A clarinet player bought a 'bass', so I had no option but to indulge in a basset-horn this month.

The total enjoyment of amateur playing has been nurtured by Benslow and all the kind and tolerant tutors who have suffered me these many years. Music is now 'my life.' I play at many venues with an assortment of groups and styles, which would not have happened if it had not been for Benslow.

Brenda Roffey

Clarinet/Viola Weekend; an interesting combination of two course run in 1995. Front row, 2nd left, John White, 2nd right, Georgina Dobree, course tutors.

Howard Davis, leader of the Alberni Quartet, tutoring Pamela Rangley.

Keeping the Flame Alive

Having taught on many Benslow weekends over many years with my quartet, the ideals and atmosphere of the organisation mean a great deal to me – particularly since my first encounter with them was in 1958 as a student. Bernard Shore was the principal coach – gentlemanly and encouraging – and the course concert was, I believe, given in the present dining room. Congratulations to all who, over the years, have kept the flame alive, through difficult times, to arrive at today's achievement.

Howard Davis (Alberni String Quartet)

INDEX OF PERSONS

SUBSCRIBERS TO BENSLOW VOICES

Juliet Abrahamson
Roy & Helen Adams
J.W. Babb
Caroline Barlow
Mr & Mrs R. Bean
Chris & Carol Beetles
Patrick & Pameli Benham
Rosemary Bennett
Nigel Billingham
Elizabeth Black
Harold Bland
Win Bland
Bernard & Nona Blay
B.J. Bolton
Geoff Booker
Sheena & Edmund Booth
Daphne Boroda
Miss M.D. Brown
Mrs Margaret Burns
Brian Butler
Norman Camomile
Gregor Campbell
Audrey Catford
Ailsa Chamberlain
Dreena Chamberlain
Penny Chilton
D. Clark
Mrs K. Clelland
Barbara Clemow
Margot Comer
Peter & Anne Conchie
Jean Cooper
Mrs Muriel Cooper
S.W. Copnell
Jane Crow
Celia Davies
Grisell Davies
Howard Davis
Miss D.E. Dormer
Phyllis Ebsworth
Anne Farquhar

Roy Ferguson
R.H. Flaxman
Tony Freeman
Gillian Gandy
Phyllida Gardner
Gillian Gifkins
Elizabeth Godfrey
P.M. Gould
M. Gray
Mary Green
Jean Harris
J.W. Hawthorn
Cyril Heels
Marie Louise Heinecke
Simon Hewitt
Lydia Hoare
Daphne Hope
Susan Hopper
H. Hornsby
Clifton Hughes
Leonard Hughes
Richard & Margaret Hughes
Ruth G. Hughes
Pam Hunter
Norman Hyde
Sonia Jackson
Edward Judge
Edward Lyons
Miss E. Lebrecht
Jean McCapra
Sue Maddex
Gill Malcolm
Andrew Marflow
Corinna Marlowe
Mrs M.O. Marrs
B.R. Meadows
Peggy Melville
Jean Middlemiss
Robin Miller
David & Monica Moore
Richard & Rosemary Moore

John Morgan
Mrs Jean Murray
David Nicholson
G. Piper
Mrs Plummer
Gill Riordan
Mrs Brenda Roffey
J.M. Rogers
Norman Routledge
Peter Saunders
Mrs Nan Scott
Madeline Seviour
Philip Shaw
Mrs E. Simpson
Mr & Mrs D.Sims
David Sheldrake
Owen Stable
Mrs Caryl Sutcliffe
T. Tanner
Christine Tenbokum
Michael Taylor
M. Turner
David Viles
Michael T. Watkins
E. Whitworth
N.B. Wickham-Irving
Richard Wiggs
Jean Williams
Michael Willoughby
Robin Woodbridge